THE PICTORIAL HISTORY
OF
SHERLOCK HOLMES

THE PICTORIAL HISTORY
OF
SHERLOCK HOLMES

MICHAEL POINTER

MALLARD
PRESS

First published in the United States
of America in 1991
by The Mallard Press
Mallard Press and its accompanying
design and logo are trademarks of
BDD Promotional Book Company,
Inc.

ISBN 0-7924-5591-6

Printed in Hong Kong

PAGE 1:
William Gillette samples a seven-per-cent solution in his play, Sherlock Holmes.

PAGES 2-3:
Frederic Dorr Steele's Holmes peers over the edge of the Reichenbach Falls.

THIS PAGE:
Dorr Steele's title page of The Adventure of the Golden Pince Nez.

CONTENTS

CHAPTER 1
THE GREAT DETECTIVE

THERE CAN BE few characters better suited as the subject of a pictorial history than Sherlock Holmes: the images of the tall figure in deerstalker and cape, or of the intense profile with pipe and lens are universally recognized, and that recognition is *literally* universal, for Sherlock Holmes is known throughout the world. This is not just because the stories by Conan Doyle have been translated and distributed worldwide; Agatha Christie's sales for example, far exceed those of Doyle, or any other fiction writer for that matter, but not even Hercule Poirot or Miss Marple have attained such recognition as Sherlock Holmes. It is the image, the actual appearance of Holmes, as well as his other attributes, that is so well-known.

In stating this, it should be understood that nothing is intended to detract from the sheer genius of Conan Doyle in creating and developing this amazing character. The result of this stroke of genius has been a personality who occupies a rightful place in that gallery of fictional immortals who have gripped the imagination of the public in a manner quite unattainable by their inferiors, and, if the truth be known, generally unexpected by their authors. The story of Conan Doyle's creation of Sherlock Holmes, modeled on his former medical tutor Dr Joseph Bell, has been related countless times and need not be repeated here at great length, but Doyle's own words on the matter are worth recalling: 'I thought of my old teacher Joe Bell, of his eagle face, of his curious ways, of his eerie trick of spotting details. If he were a detective he would surely reduce this fascinating but unorganized business to something nearer to an exact science. I would try if I could get this effect. It was surely possible in real life, so why should I not make it plausible in fiction? It is all very well to say a man is clever, but the reader wants to see examples of it – such examples as Bell have us every day in the wards. The idea amused me. What should I call the fellow? . . . First it was

Sherringford Holmes; then it was Sherlock Holmes . . . He could not tell his own exploits, so he must have a commonplace comrade as a foil – an educated man of action who could both join in the exploits and narrate them. A drab, quiet name for this unostentatious man. Watson would do. And so I had my puppets and wrote my *Study in Scarlet.'*

"The Adventure of the Three Students"

ABOVE:
*The stern figure with pointing hand and dramatic shadow in profile,
and the oil lamp and books, are the only elements necessary in this
striking composition by Frederic Dorr Steele, drawn for the cover of*
Collier's Weekly, *24 September 1904.*

LEFT:
*The first Sherlock Holmes story was reprinted by Ward Lock as a
supplement to the* Windsor Magazine *Christmas Number for 1895,
with this rather lurid cover.*

However, it has to be acknowledged that for all Conan Doyle's masterly invention in the creation of Sherlock Holmes, the immense popularity of the great detective has been greatly assisted and maintained first by the illustrators to the stories and secondly by the impersonators of Holmes in the hundreds of dramatizations that have been made over a period of almost a century. Not only did the first two Sherlock Holmes stories, *A Study in Scarlet* and *The Sign of Four*, have merely a modest reception by the public, but they suffered from mediocre to downright poor illustrations. The first Sherlock Holmes story, *A Study in Scarlet*, was published by Ward Lock, who had acquired the business of Samuel Beeton; his best-known publications were his wife's celebrated cookery books, yet *Beeton's Christmas Annual* for 1887 is now extremely valuable because of the appearance of 'the world's first consulting detective', as he styled himself. The first publication of the story in print was a landmark, giving us Doyle's description of Sherlock Holmes – 'rather over six feet . . . excessively lean . . . sharp and piercing eyes . . . thin hawk-like nose', but the simultaneous first illustration, by D H Friston, did nothing at all for Sherlock Holmes, and Dr Watson looks pretty dreary with an excess of facial hair. The pictures were not a success, and really neither was the story.

LEFT:
The elaborate reproduction of the Baker Street consulting room, at the Château de Lucens, Switzerland in 1968.

RIGHT:
The second edition of A Study in Scarlet, *and first appearance in book form, was illustrated by the author's father, Charles Doyle.*

BELOW:
The very first depiction of the Great Detective was by D H Friston in Beeton's Christmas Annual.

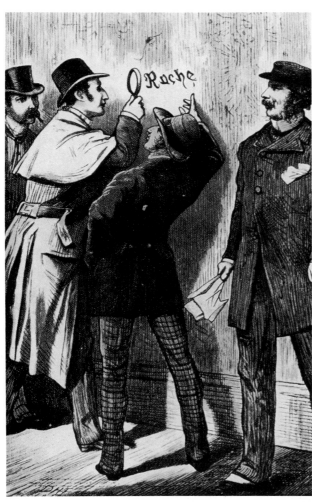

RIGHT:
William Gillette, caricatured in the magazine Vanity Fair.

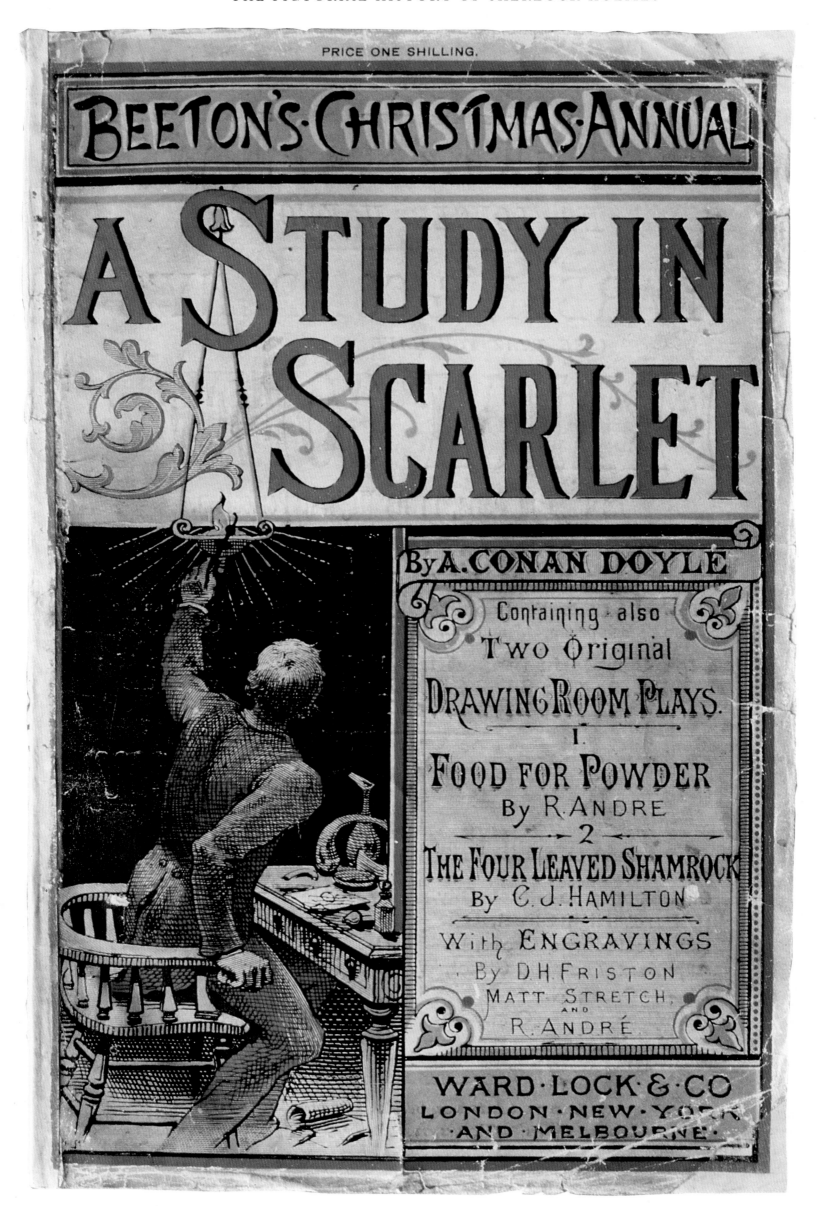

LEFT:

The most famous and most scarce of all Sherlock Holmes covers – the first appearance of the first title, as revealed to an unsuspecting public in 1887. In June 1990 a copy was sold in New York for $52,000.

RIGHT:

Dr Joseph Bell, Conan Doyle's acknowledged model for many of the characteristics of Sherlock Holmes.

ABOVE:

The extent to which the Sherlock Holmes stories were used to sell The Strand Magazine can be seen in these covers from the 1920s.

According to Winifred Paget, the editor intended to commission her uncle Walter Paget to produce the illustrations to Doyle's stories, but wrote to her father Sydney Paget by mistake. This happy accident has been compared with the chance collaboration of Laurel and Hardy, or Basil Rathbone and Nigel Bruce, and surely a more suitable combination could never have been arranged by design. The late James Montgomery, an American expert on Sherlock Holmes illustrations, justly remarked, 'What Phiz did for Pickwick, Paget did for Sherlock Holmes.'

The first six stories, charmingly embellished with Sidney Paget's pictures, were an immediate success, and hasty arrangements were made for a further six to complete the dozen, still with Sidney Paget as artist. Unwittingly, Conan Doyle and Greenhough Smith between them had invented the crime series – and without this format where would television drama be today? The series ran in *The Strand* from July 1891 to June 1892, and there can be no doubt that Greenhough Smith could see what an important contribution Paget's drawings made to the stories' success, for when the further series *Memoirs of Sherlock Holmes* finished in *The Strand* in 1893, a new series of stories by Arthur Morrison called *Martin Hewitt, Investigator* was begun, and again Paget was engaged to provide the illustrations.

In all Sidney Paget illustrated 38 of the Sherlock Holmes stories in *The Strand*, and was only prevented from continuing to do so by his untimely death in 1908. By that

Three years later, in February 1890, the second story, *The Sign of Four*, was published in *Lippincott's Monthly Magazine*. This time Sherlock Holmes was not depicted at all, and the story met with an equally modest reception from the public. There the matter could have ended, and the two stories would probably have been classified as minor late-Victorian novels of crime and detection. Happily, a fortuitous combination of circumstances ensued: George Newnes launched a new magazine, and Dr Conan Doyle, having given up medicine and taken up writing for a living, needed the money, and offered to write for it.

George Newnes deserves the credit for producing *The Strand Magazine*, the best quality monthly magazine of its kind, and the editor, Greenhough Smith, the credit for accepting a series of six short stories by Doyle, under the heading *The Adventures of Sherlock Holmes*. At this point the third factor in the combination of circumstances became effective.

ABOVE:
*Conan Doyle towards the end of his life and (right) Sidney Paget, The
Strand's most celebrated illustrator*

BELOW:
*Some of Paget's best pictures illustrated the story Silver Blaze. Here,
Holmes and Watson are met at the railway station by their client and
a police inspector and (right) Holmes delivers a straight left.*

ABOVE & BELOW:
Two quintessential Paget illustrations, both beautifully drawn and engraved, showing Holmes and Watson in typical settings.

time his grand total of 356 illustrations had set a standard which his successors had to try and follow, and by which all subsequent illustrators are now measured. He not only delineated the detective's features in what became the generally accepted appearance of Sherlock Holmes, but he was responsible for depicting him in what is now the first Holmesian trademark – the deerstalker hat. As early as the fourth of the *Adventures*, when Dr Watson refers to Holmes's close-fitting cloth cap', Paget drew what he often wore himself – a deerstalker.

Looking back, it seems that the success of *The Strand Magazine* was as much due to the popularity of the Sherlock Holmes stories as the success of the stories was due to *The Strand*. The complementary nature of this achievement was not lost on Greenhough Smith, whose reading public was clamoring for more tales of the great detective, and Smith repeatedly urged Conan Doyle to produce more. By this time Doyle was getting into his stride as an author, and had his sights set on what he felt were more worthy subjects. In the end he agreed to another dozen stories, but he was determined that they would be the last. This second series was called *The Memoirs of Sherlock Holmes* and in the first story, *Silver Blaze*, Sidney Paget again portrayed Sherlock Holmes wearing a deerstalker. In all other illustrations, both then and later, Holmes was shown wearing the conventional soft felt hat or topper, as the occasion required. At the end of *The Memoirs*,

Doyle carried out his stated intention (in a letter to his mother) of getting rid of Holmes, so that he could get on with what he regarded as far more important work, his historical novels. In *The Final Problem* Holmes confronts the master-criminal Professor Moriarty and the two perish in the dramatic death struggle at the Reichenbach Falls.

The outcry from the reading public was tremendous, and George Newnes, apprehensive of the effect on his magazine's sales, reported the death of Sherlock Holmes to his shareholders as 'a dreadful event.' For over seven years Conan Doyle resisted all efforts to persuade him to produce further Holmes tales, for he was busy turning out a stream of stories and novels of other kinds; in the meantime a hugely successful stage play entitled *Sherlock Holmes* had been presented in America by the actor/dramatist William Gillette, who appeared in the title role. Gillette brought the play to England in September 1901 where it was equally successful, and since he had adopted a deerstalker as part of his costume in the play, it comes as no surprise that when the short stories resumed in

The Strand Magazine in October 1903, five of them contained Paget illustrations that featured that 'ear-flapped traveling cap', as Watson described it (the word 'deerstalker' does not occur in any of the stories).

The success of Gillette's play in America and its subsequent transfer to England revived the demands on Conan Doyle for further Sherlock Holmes stories, and having received the idea for a chilling mystery story, or 'creeper' as he termed it, he decided to frame it in the form of a Sherlock Holmes adventure that supposedly had taken place before the detective's demise. The story was *The Hound of the Baskervilles*, serialized in *The Strand* from August 1902, and this time Conan Doyle particularly requested that the illustrations should be by Sidney Paget. It was a time of the most intense popularity of Sherlock Holmes in Britain, for just as the serial ended there were no fewer than seven companies touring simultaneously in various Sherlock Holmes stage plays. Small wonder then that the pressure on Conan Doyle to resume the Holmes stories increased still further. When the American

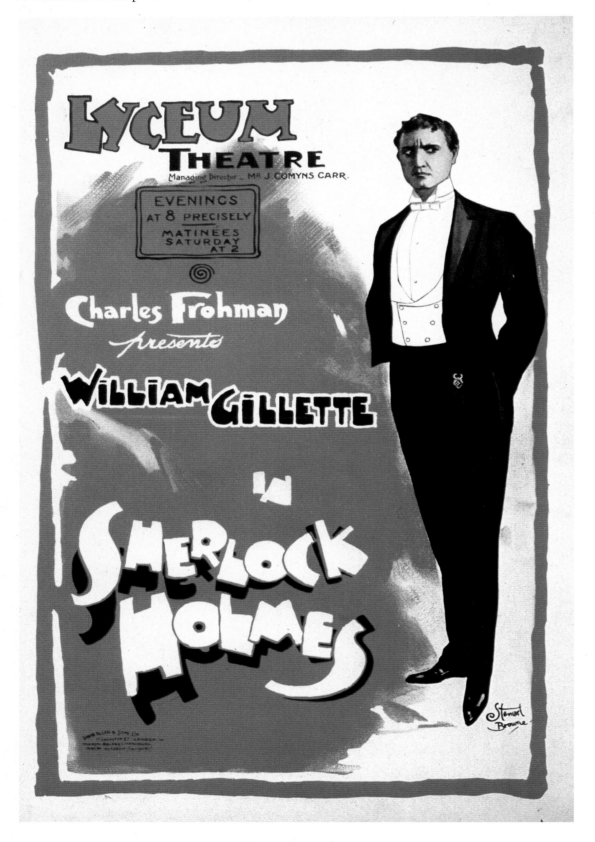

LEFT:
William Gillette appeared in his play Sherlock Holmes *at the Lyceum Theatre, London, from September 1901 to April 1902.*

ABOVE:
Paget's depiction of the climax of
The Hound of the Baskervilles.

BELOW:
*The master criminal Professor
Moriarty, drawn by Sidney Paget.*

RIGHT:
*Two more of Frederic Dorr Steele's
outstanding cover pictures for*
Collier's Weekly, *for December
1904 and January 1905.*

THE ADVENTURE
of the
ABBEY GRANGE

The
Last Adventure
of
Sherlock Holmes

in this number

Vol XXXIV No 18   JANUARY 28 1905   PRICE 10 CENTS

ABOVE LEFT:
'The tall and portly form of Mycroft Holmes,' together with Holmes and Watson, in a fine picture by Arthur Twidle, 1908.

ABOVE:
H M Brock produced this highly effective illustration for The Red Circle in 1911.

LEFT:
An unused portrait of Sherlock Holmes by Sidney Paget, first published in 1951.

magazine *Collier's Weekly* offered him $45,000 for 13 new Holmes tales, and *The Strand Magazine* made a substantial offer for the British rights as well, he finally gave in. In *Collier's Weekly* on 26 September 1903, and in *The Strand* for October 1903, the story *The Empty House* inaugurated the new series of 13 tales called *The Return of Sherlock Holmes*. Holmes, it appeared, had not really gone over the Reichenbach Falls, but was forced to conceal his survival from Watson, who could not be relied upon to pretend convincingly that his friend was dead, and so might inadvertently give the game away to Moriarty's second-in-command who, unlike the rest of the Professor's evil gang, had eluded capture.

With the extraordinary demand for further stories enabling Conan Doyle to command exceptional fees, he was also in a much stronger position to exercise control, and after *The Return* series ended in 1905 there was neither a regular appear-

ance of the stories, nor in Britain a regular illustrator, for Sidney Paget had died in 1908. The final 20 Sherlock Holmes stories were spread over 22 years, ending in 1927. Every story from *Adventures* onward was first published in Britain in *The Strand Magazine*, and with the tradition of 13 years of Sidney Paget illustrations before them, the subsequent illustrators in *The Strand* had no choice but to attempt to perpetuate Paget's visual conception of Holmes and Watson, albeit in their own styles.

Paget's successor as illustrator was Arthur Twidle, who was also responsible for some excellent pictures in the books of collected stories, and he was followed by Gilbert Holiday, H M Brock and others, until in 1914 the splendid Frank Wiles was commissioned to illustrate the nine instalments of *The Valley of Fear*. He began with an incomparable colored frontispiece of Sherlock Holmes's head in

RIGHT:
*A less sharply defined Holmes and
Watson in* The Devil's Foot, *by
Gilbert Holiday, 1910.*

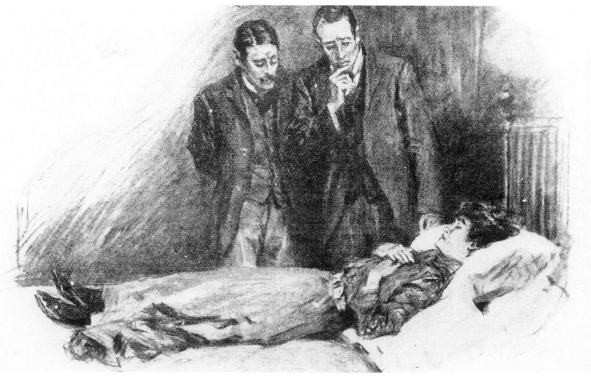

RIGHT:
*A less sharply defined Holmes and
Watson in* The Devil's Foot, *by
Gilbert Holiday, 1910.*

STRAND
MAGAZINE
SHERLOCK HOLMES AGAIN!

15 Cents

LEFT:
*Joseph Simpson's illustration for
The Red Circle in The Strand
Magazine of March 1911 was
reproduced in color on the cover of
the American version of the same
magazine one month later.*

profile, the only time a color illustration to the stories was used inside *The Strand.* It also fell to Frank Wiles to provide the pictures for the three Holmes stories that Conan Doyle wrote in 1927; for the third of these, and for no explained reason, Wiles re-introduced the deerstalker as Holmes's headgear. It had not once been depicted in *The Strand* since Sidney Paget had illustrated *Black Peter* in March 1904, and its use by Frank Wiles in *Shoscombe Old Place* in April 1927 has been regarded by some as prophetic, for Conan Doyle died in 1931. It was the last Sherlock Holmes story.

ABOVE & BELOW:
Three of the impressive illustrations to Shoscombe Old Place *by Frank Wiles, 1927.*

Holmes released the spaniel, and with a joyous cry it dashed forward to the carriage and sprang upon the step.

"I also have a question to ask you, Sir Robert," said Holmes in his sternest tone. "Who is this? And what is it doing here?"

THE ADVENTURE
of the
MISSING THREE-QUARTER

VOL XXXIV No 9   NOVEMBER 26   PRICE 10 CENTS

ABOVE:
*'The dog sniffed round for an
instant, and then . . . started off
down the street tugging at his leash
in his efforts to go faster.' Frederic
Dorr Steele's cover picture for*
Collier's Weekly, *November 1904.*

In America the enthusiasm for Sherlock Holmes did not become widespread quite so early, although it has now surpassed that of any other nation. The first printings of the stories were in a haphazard order, in a variety of newspapers and weekly periodicals, and the illustrations were equally irregular, and mostly unsatisfactory. It was not until the series *The Return of Sherlock Holmes* began in *Collier's Weekly* in September 1903, with color cover pictures by Frederic Dorr Steele, that an American perception of the appearance of Sherlock Holmes emerged, and it was based, as Steele himself

was the first to admit, on the actor William Gillette's appearance as Holmes. The features, and often the poses, were copied by the artist from photographs of the actor, and are only really fully satisfying if one favors the appearance of Gillette as Holmes.

Steele illustrated two more of the stories for *Collier's* after *The Return* series, and a further 14 for other American magazines, but this impressive collection of work has been little known in Britain and Europe, just as Sidney Paget's work has only been known from three of the Holmes stories that

LEFT:
The worldwide recognition of Sherlock Holmes's great powers is exhibited by these early letters addressed to him from the USA and Bosnia-Herzegovina. Some stuffy Post Office official has endorsed the first envelope: 'If this letter is intended for Dr Conan Doyle it should be so addressed.'

9 Eriswell Road,

Worthing.

18th Novr 1904.

Dear Sir,

I trust I am not trespassing too much on your time and kindness by asking for the favour of your autograph to add to my collection.

I have derived very much pleasure from reading your Memoirs, and should very highly value the possession of your famous signature.

Trusting you will see your way to thus honour me, and venturing to thank you very much in anticipation,

I am, Sir,

Your obedient Servant,

Charles Wright

P.S. Not being aware of your present address, I am taking the liberty of sending this letter to Sir A. Conan Doyle, asking him to be good enough to forward it to you.

Sherlock Holmes Esq.

ABOVE & LEFT:
Fact or fiction? The confusion in many minds as to the reality of Sherlock Holmes is exemplified in these letters of 1904, two of many hundreds of similar epistles.

appeared in the American edition of *The Strand*, together with a random selection of Paget's other pictures.

Thus until comparatively recently there have been separate and somewhat differing American and British conventions as to the accepted appearance of the world's greatest detective.

Frederic Dorr Steele, with the advantage of the eleven colored cover pictures that he drew for *Collier's Weekly*, achieved an impact denied to any other illustrator of Sherlock Holmes stories, with the possible exception of Robert Faw-

cett, mentioned later. In addition, Steele's pictures for *The Return* series were later syndicated in a number of major American newspapers, giving the artist's work an even wider exposure. Looking at these pictures now, it seems that Steele poured so much of his talent into the color cover pictures that the black-and-white illustrations within the text of the stories emerged as very variable from the barely adequate to the strikingly atmospheric and appropriate. Only one of the 11 cover pictures that accompanied *The Return* series did not depict Sherlock Holmes, and that was the starkly dramatic picture of

The Sherlock Holmes Journal

VOL. 12, No. 2 (FORTY-SIXTH ISSUE)   WINTER 1975

Published by the Sherlock Holmes Society of London

PRINCIPAL CONTENTS

ABOVE & RIGHT:
Note the use of Sidney Paget illustrations on three of the four record sleeves containing radio broadcasts.

LEFT:
The British Sherlock Holmes Journal *carries on its cover an adaptation of a* Strand Magazine *illustration by Howard K Elcock, whereas the American* Baker Street Journal *(right) loyally bears a portrait head of Holmes by Dorr Steele.*

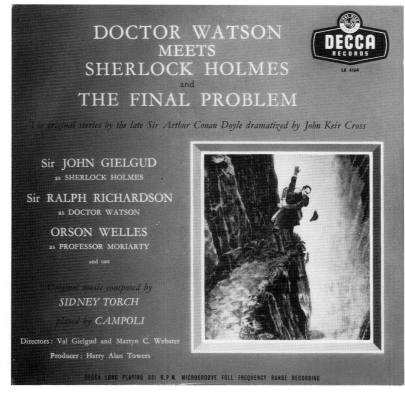

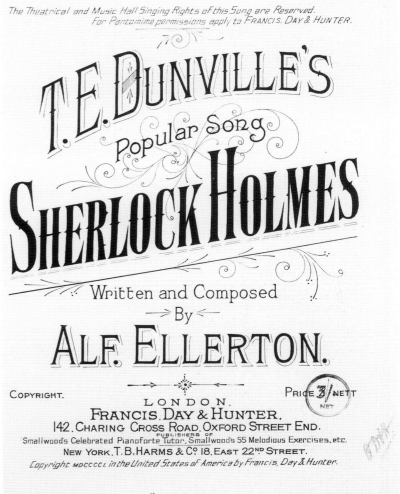

ABOVE:
*Probably unknown to Conan Doyle,
there were several music-hall songs
extolling the characteristics of
Sherlock Holmes. This one dates
from 1901.*

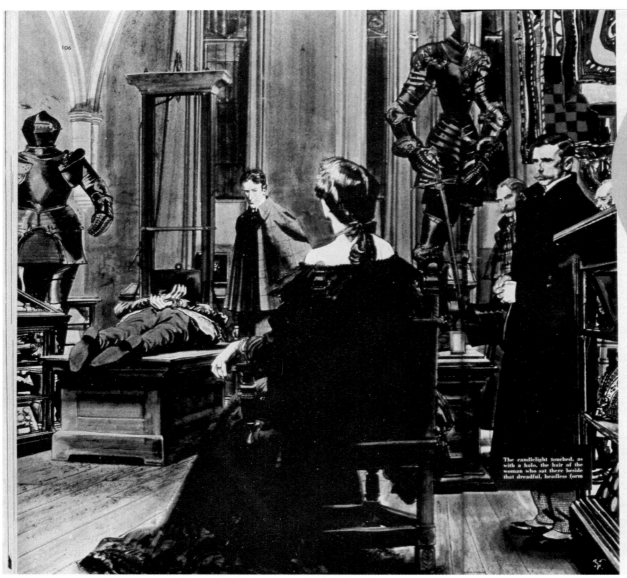

The Adventure of the RED WIDOW

By ADRIAN CONAN DOYLE

A man was beheaded, and another man had vanished. To the police it was obvious who the murderer was—but Sherlock Holmes had another idea

"YOUR conclusions are perfectly correct, my dear Watson," remarked my friend Sherlock Holmes. "Squalor and poverty are the natural matrix for crimes of violence."

"Precisely so," I agreed. "Indeed, I was just thinking—" I broke off to stare at him in amazement. "Good heavens, Holmes," I cried, "this is too much. How could you possibly know my innermost thoughts!"

My friend leaned back in his chair and, placing his finger tips together, surveyed me from under his heavy drooping eyelids. "I would do better justice to my limited powers, perhaps, by refusing to answer your question," he said, with a dry chuckle. "You have a certain flair, Watson, for concealing your failure to perceive the obvious by the cavalier manner in which you invariably accept the explanation of a sequence of simple but logical reasoning."

"I do not see how logical reasoning can enable you to follow the course of my mental processes," I retorted, a trifle nettled by his superior manner.

"There was no great difficulty. I have been watching you for the last few minutes. The expression on your face was quite vacant until, as your eyes roved around the room, they fell on the bookcase and came to rest on Hugo's Les Misérables, which made so deep an impression upon you when you read it last year. You became thoughtful; your eyes narrowed.

The candlelight touched, as with a halo, the hair of the woman who sat there beside that dreadful, headless form

Another New Sherlock Holmes Story

THIS STORY IS PRINTED BY ARRANGEMENT WITH THE ESTATE OF THE LATE SIR ARTHUR CONAN DOYLE. COPYRIGHT 1952 BY ADRIAN CONAN DOYLE

ILLUSTRATED BY ROBERT FAWCETT

The Adventure of the DEPTFORD HORROR

By ADRIAN CONAN DOYLE

Three members of one family had been murdered— two remained. If Holmes failed, tomorrow there would be only one

I HAVE remarked elsewhere that my friend Sherlock Holmes, like all great artists, lived for his art's sake and, save in the case of the Duke of Holdernesse, I have seldom known him to claim any substantial reward. However powerful or wealthy the client, he would refuse to undertake any problem that lacked appeal to his sympathies, while he would devote his most intense energies to the affairs of some humble person whose case contained those singular and bizarre qualities which struck a responsive chord in his imagination.

On glancing through my notes for that memorable year of 1895, I find recorded the details of a case which may be taken as a typical instance of this disinterested and even altruistic attitude of his which placed the rendering of a kindly service above that of material reward. I refer to the dreadful affair of the canaries and the soot marks on the ceiling.

It was early in June that my friend completed his investigations into the sudden death of Cardinal Tosca, an inquiry which he had undertaken at the special request of the pope. The case had demanded the most exacting work on Holmes's part and, as I had feared at the time, the aftermath had left him in a highly nervous and restless state that caused me some concern both as his friend and his medical adviser.

One rainy night toward the end of the same month, I persuaded him to dine with me at Frascatti's and thereafter we had gone on to the Café Royal for our coffee and liqueurs. As I had hoped, the bustle of the great room with its red plush seats and stately palms bathed in the glow of numerous crystal chandeliers drew him out of his introspective mood. As he leaned back on our sofa, his fingers playing with the stem of his glass, I noted with satisfaction a gleam of interest in those keen gray eyes as he studied the somewhat Bohemian clientele that thronged the tables and alcoves.

I was in the act of replying to some remark when Holmes nodded suddenly in the direction of the door. "Lestrade," said he. "What can he be doing here?"

Glancing over my shoulder, I saw the lean rat-faced figure of the Scotland Yard man standing in the entrance, his dark eyes looking slowly

Red, beady eyes shone at us in the light with a baleful iridescence. "Watson! Don't move!" whispered Holmes, a note of horror in his voice

Another New Sherlock Holmes Story

THIS STORY IS PRINTED BY ARRANGEMENT WITH THE ESTATE OF THE LATE SIR ARTHUR CONAN DOYLE. COPYRIGHT 1952 BY ADRIAN CONAN DOYLE

ILLUSTRATED BY ROBERT FAWCETT

the titled lady who shoots Charles Augustus Milverton, in the story of that name. Even in the ten covers that feature Holmes, his appearance varies from alert and slightly grizzled to haggard and grey, the least attractive being that for *The Priory School*, a poor representation of Gillette's stance and appearance.

In recent years, however, the publication of facsimile reproductions of the work of both Paget and Steele has enabled each of them to become better known and appreciated in the other's country. In 1987 the American scholar Andrew Malec made the following shrewd observations: 'During the first 40 years of this century, few Americans could think of Sherlock Holmes without calling to mind the features of William Gillette and the illustrations of Frederic Dorr Steele. Following Steele's death, however, their dual influence began to wane, even in the United States. Basil Rathbone became the average person's mental picture of the detective . . . he represented a return to the Paget model of Holmes.'

Just 50 years after Steele began his Sherlock Holmes illustrations, in 1953, *Colliers* again established a landmark with the engagement of Robert Fawcett, who produced a series of spectacular illustrations to *The Exploits of Sherlock Holmes*, for which one can give nothing but enthusiastic admiration. With just one large color picture per story, Fawcett captured the heavy atmosphere and rich flavor of the late Victorian era, and illuminated the texts in a manner and style of high quality. It remains a matter of great regret that he was never commissioned to illustrate an edition of the original Arthur Conan Doyle stories, for *The Exploits* were short stories written by Conan Doyle's son Adrian, in collaboration with the eminent American mystery story author John Dickson Carr.

LEFT:
Two of Robert Fawcett's magnificent pictures that illuminated The Exploits of Sherlock Holmes *in* Colliers' *in 1953.*

ABOVE RIGHT:
The last Sherlock Holmes story in The Strand Magazine *was* The Adventure of the First Class Carriage *by Ronald Knox, illustrated by Tom Purvis in the style of Sidney Paget.*

RIGHT:
Seated on a boulder in the village of Meiringen, within sight of the Reichenbach Falls, this bronze statue of the Great Detective by John Doubleday was unveiled in 1988.

CHAPTER 2
THE GREAT IMPERSONATORS ON THE STAGE

THE DISTINCTION OF being the first person known to have impersonated Sherlock Holmes anywhere in the world fell to Charles Brookfield, an irreverent satirist who, like many young rebels, eventually became a part of the Establishment; he ended up as Lord Chamberlain, responsible for (among other things) curbing the stage excesses of rebellious and irreverent satirists. Brookfield joined with Seymour Hicks in concocting what was effectively the first 'revue' to be presented on the English stage, entitled *Under the Clock*, first performed 25 November 1893. In addition to making fun of a number of theatrical personalities of the day, the piece guyed Holmes and Watson in several ways, including Watson's adoration of Holmes's skill and methods ('Oh! Sherlock, you wonderful man!' went one refrain).

The first drama proper that featured Sherlock Holmes was an unauthorized play by Charles Rogers entitled *Sherlock Holmes*. At that time Conan Doyle had no copyright protection against such piracy and, in fact, Rogers secured for himself what was then termed a 'playright' for his play by giving it a so-called copyright performance (under the title *Sherlock Holmes, Private Detective*) in December 1893, less than a month after *Under the Clock* was produced. Charles Rogers's play was then formally launched in May 1894, with John Webb in the title role. It was a lurid melodrama of a type that was very popular in the touring circuit theaters of the late Victorian era, and although not of exceptional quality it survived to travel the British provinces for at least ten years, as well as touring South Africa. During that time there had appeared in America, and then in Britain, the play also called *Sherlock Holmes* by the American actor William Gillette.

Sometime during the late 1890s Conan Doyle had written a Sherlock Holmes play that was never staged. It eventually ended up in the hands of William Gillette, who

ABOVE:
Brookfield wrote a line from the first song in Under the Clock *on this photograph, printed in Upper Baker Street.*

RIGHT:
William Gillette as Sherlock Holmes in a reverie, visualizing characters from the play.

26

must have thought so little of it that he rewrote it, making sure that it highlighted his own acting talents. As nothing of Doyle's play appears to have survived, it is impossible to know how much Gillette actually altered. It seems fairly clear that there was little or no love interest in the original script, for Gillette himself recounted in an interview printed in *The Strand Magazine*, that he had written to Conan Doyle requesting permission to take various liberties with the leading character; he plainly had in mind a romance involving Sherlock Holmes. Doyle, having gone to some lengths to rid himself of the character whose popularity had threatened the output of his other writings, was quite unconcerned as to the treatment of Holmes, and recalled the episode in his autobiography:

'It was written and most wonderfully acted by William Gillette, the famous American. Since he used my characters and to some extent my plots, he naturally gave me a share in the undertaking, which proved to be very successful. "May I marry Holmes?" was one cable which I received from him when in the throes of composition. "You may marry or murder or do what you like with him," was my heartless reply. I was charmed both with the play, the acting and the pecuniary result.'

Gillette was extremely experienced in melodrama and, knowing that a romantic element would widen the appeal of the play, had Sherlock Holmes fall in love with the heroine; at the finale the curtain fell on the extraordinary sight of the pair embracing in the limelight. It was extraordinary because from the 14 stories that had been published at that time it was quite apparent that Holmes, the methodical calculating and reasoning machine, had no time for any such subjective emotions. But Gillette's judgement was sound, and audiences took to the play with enormous pleasure, first in the USA, then in Britain and eventually in many other parts of the world. It opened in Buffalo in 1899, and after a huge success in New York and

William Gillette

ABOVE:
This photograph seems to personify Gillette's somber and slightly over-dignified portrayal of Sherlock Holmes.

LEFT:
Sherlock Holmes and Alice Faulkner in the romantic close to Gillette's play.

RIGHT:
Although Sherlock Holmes's dressing gown is referred to in the Doyle stories from time to time, Gillette deserves the credit, or disrepute if you will, for introducing this extravagant, quilted brocade garment.

LEFT:
The famous scene of confrontation between the Great Detective and the Napoleon of Crime, as presented in Gillette's gripping play.

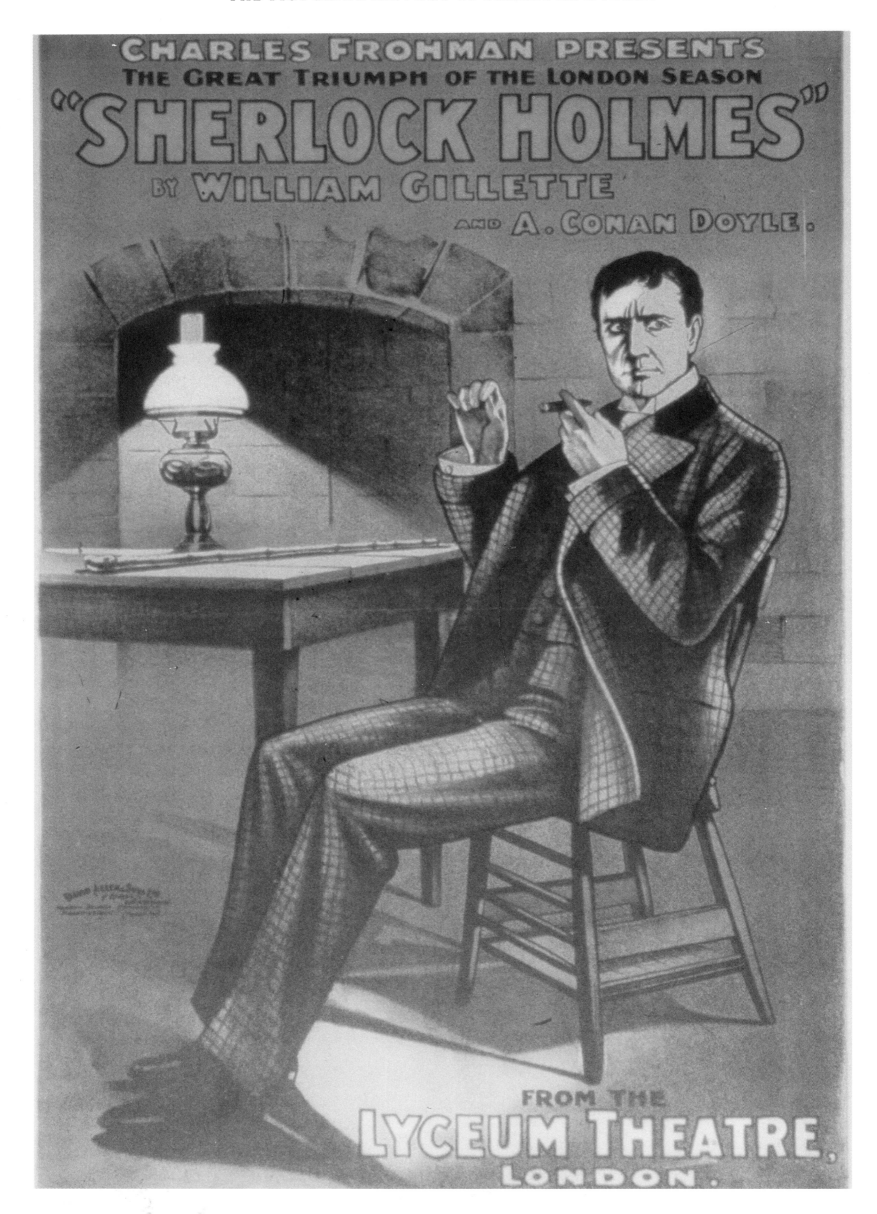

LEFT:
A poster for the William Gillette play adapted for use by touring companies in Britain.

RIGHT:
The languid Holmes of William Gillette relaxes once Moriarty and his henchman have been handcuffed.

elsewhere in the USA came to England in September 1901, bringing with it a reputation for its highly dramatic special effects. Gillette's rather stiff and dignified portrayal of Sherlock Holmes, coupled with an initial lack of voice projection within the Lyceum Theater, was not at first well received, but his personality and his commitment to the role overcame these difficulties, and the great American success was repeated in London. This was followed by an eight-week tour of Britain before returning to the USA to further and continuing popularity. Initially it was the combination of Gillette in his own play that was so successful, and it is obvious that Gillette had created the piece to present himself in the best possible light. He had done it so well that it proved to be the greatest triumph of his career, but the strong drama that had been constructed from several of the Doyle stories was so effective that many other actors were also able to enjoy great triumphs in it, and it had an amazingly long life for a melodrama. Numerous translations of Gillette's *Sherlock Holmes* were produced in Europe and overseas, and various touring companies took the

play on the road around the world, over many years.

In the meantime Conan Doyle himself had written another stage play featuring Sherlock Holmes in 1910. It came about because Doyle had earlier composed a play called *The House of Temperley*, based on his own novel *Rodney Stone*, but had been unable to find a backer for it. He rashly decided to finance it himself, and leased the Adelphi Theater for six months. Unfortunately *The House of Temperley* failed, and to retrieve the situation Doyle turned to Sherlock Holmes, a tacit recognition of the character's certain popularity. He wrote *The Speckled Band*, based on his own short story of that name, first printed in 1892, and, as he described it: 'Before the end of the run I had cleared off all that I had lost upon the other play, and I had created a permanent property of some value.'

This 'permanent property' was subtitled 'An Adventure of Sherlock Holmes', an important factor in the publicity, and had H A Saintsbury as Sherlock Holmes. Saintsbury was no stranger to the role, having already toured in the William Gillette play for three years, and his sober and restrained per-

Duke of York's Theatre

ST MARTIN'S LANE WC

Proprietors ... ... Mr & Mrs Frank Wyatt

Sole Lessee and Manager ... ... CHARLES FROHMAN

CHARLES FROHMAN PRESENTS
A DRAMA IN FOUR ACTS
BY A. CONAN DOYLE
AND WILLIAM GILLETTE
ENTITLED

SHERLOCK HOLMES

BEING A HITHERTO UNPUBLISHED EPISODE
IN THE CAREER OF THE GREAT DETECTIVE
AND SHOWING HIS CONNECTION WITH THE

STRANGE CASE OF MISS FAULKNER

CHARACTERS IN THE PLAY	COMPANY APPEARING IN THE CAST
SHERLOCK HOLMES	WILLIAM GILLETTE
DOCTOR WATSON ...	KENNETH RIVINGTON
JOHN FORMAN ...	EUGENE MAYEUR
SIR EDWARD LEIGHTON ...	REGINALD DANCE
COUNT VON STAHLBURG ...	FREDERICK MORRIS
PROFESSOR MORIARTY	GEORGE SUMNER
JAMES LARRABEE ...	FRANCIS CARLYLE
SIDNEY PRINCE	QUINTON McPHERSON
ALFRED BASSICK ...	WILLIAM H. DAY
JIM CRAIGIN ...	CHRIS WALKER
THOMAS LEARY ...	HENRY WALTERS
"LIGHTFOOT" McTAGUE ...	WALTER DISON
JOHN	THOMAS QUINTON
PARSONS	G. MERTON
BILLY ...	CHARLES CHAPLIN
ALICE FAULKNER	MARIE DORO
MRS. FAULKNER ...	DE OLIA WEBSTER
MADGE LARRABEE	ADELAIDE PRINCE
THERESE ...	SYBIL CAMPBELL
MRS. SMEEDLEY	ETHEL LORRIMORE

THE PLACE IS LONDON
THE TIME TEN YEARS AGO

FIRST ACT—DRAWING ROOM AT THE LARRABEES'—EVENING

SECOND ACT—Scene I—PROFESSOR MORIARTY'S
UNDERGROUND OFFICE—MORNING

Scene II—SHERLOCK HOLMES' APARTMENTS
IN BAKER STREET—EVENING

THIRD ACT—THE STEPNEY GAS CHAMBER—MIDNIGHT

FOURTH ACT—DOCTOR WATSON'S CONSULTING ROOM KENSINGTON—THE
FOLLOWING EVENING

SCENERY BY ERNEST GROS INCIDENTAL MUSIC BY WILLIAM FURST

INTERMISSIONS

Between the 1st and 2nd Acts, 9 minutes
Between the 2nd and 3rd Acts, 7 minutes
Between the 3rd and 4th Acts, 8 minutes

MATINEE every Saturday at 2.15 o'clock

BUSINESS MANAGER—JAMES W MATHEWS ACTING MANAGER—ROBERT M EBERLE
STAGE MANAGER—WILLIAM POSTANCE . MUSICAL DIRECTOR—JOHN CROOK

ABOVE:

*When William Gillette revived the
play in London in 1905, he sent for
young Charles Chaplin who had
been touring in the provinces in the
role of Billy. 'I trembled with
anxiety,' wrote Chaplin, 'for it was
doubtful if our Company could
replace Billy at such short notice.'*

LEFT:

*H A Saintsbury, who toured British
theaters as Holmes in the Gillette
play, and who gave Chaplin his
first chance on the legitimate stage.*

RIGHT:

*Saintsbury also played Holmes in
Conan Doyle's play The Speckled
Band in 1910.*

formance in the part was soundly based on Gillette's interpretation of Holmes. For part of his touring career in Gillette's play, Saintsbury had been accompanied by the young Charles Chaplin, whom he had engaged as Billy, the Baker Street page boy, a part which Chaplin carried with great distinction, and for which he was always grateful to Saintsbury.

The Speckled Band as a play suffered from the same difficulty as the Charles Rogers play and other melodramas of the time in that the villain of the piece proved to be a much stronger character dramatically than Sherlock Holmes, and thus unbalanced the play. In spite of this it had a considerable success, and enjoyed several revivals and tours, both in Britain and America. Conan Doyle's only other venture in putting Holmes on the stage was a one-act play called *The Crown Diamond* in 1921. This was a curiosity as, unusually, he later adapted the play as a short story.

Apart from minor piracies and imitations, Gillette's play and Doyle's *Speckled Band* occupied the field until the theater was greatly diminished by the rise of the cinema. There were a few exceptions, but none achieved an outstanding success. In 1923 *The Return of Sherlock Holmes*, featuring Eille Norwood as Holmes, was really capitalizing on the

CRIMINALS, BEWARE THE HAWK-LIKE EYE!

THE UNDYING SHERLOCK HOLMES: MR. SAINTSBURY'S REPRESENTATION OF THE NAPOLEON OF DETECTIVES
IN "THE SPECKLED BAND," AT THE ADELPHI.

In his representation of Sir Arthur Conan Doyle's famous character, Mr. H. A. Saintsbury has, it will be seen, based his make-up closely on the late Mr. Sidney Paget's illustrations to the stories as they appeared in the "Strand Magazine." Dressing-gown, pipe, and all the other familiar accessories are there. Mr. Saintsbury also thoroughly looks the part, and he has had considerable experience in playing it in the provinces before the piece was put on in London. It may be recalled that the title-part in "Sherlock Holmes" was first played in London at the Lyceum in 1901 by Mr. William Gillette, who had previously produced that play in New York.

Photographs by Ellis and Walery.

huge success he had enjoyed in no fewer than 47 silent films. A decade later, in 1933, Felix Aylmer was an elderly retired Holmes attempting to cope with a brilliant daughter named Shirley (what else?) in *The Holmeses of Baker Street*, a highly original and clever play which unfortunately did not succeed. A much more ambitious presentation was the musical *Baker Street*, which ran for almost a year in New York in 1965, but which because of enormous costs was still a financial failure, and was never staged in Britain.

The popularity of first the silent films, and then the sound films and television plays, had made it highly unlikely that there would be any further grand scale appearances of Sherlock Holmes on the stage. Consequently it was a great and welcome surprise when the Royal Shakespeare Company presented a splendidly mounted revival of the old William Gillette play at the Aldwych Theater, London, in 1973, for there had been no major production of a Sherlock Holmes play on the London stage for 40 years. Even more surprising

MR. PUNCH'S PERSONALITIES.

XII.—SIR ARTHUR CONAN DOYLE.

YOUR own creation, that great sleuth
Who spent his life in chasing Truth—
How does he view your late defiance
(O ARTHUR!) of the laws of Science?

He disapproves your strange vagaries,
Your spooks and photographs of fairies;
And holds you foot-cuffed when you're fain
To navigate the vast inane.

We sympathise with *Holmes*; and yet
In *Punch's* heart your name is set;
Of every DOYLE he's still a lover
For DICKY'S sake, who did his cover.

ABOVE:
*Bernard Partridge neatly delineated the way in which, by the end of his
life, Conan Doyle had become shackled to his most famous character.*

LEFT:
Jarmila Novotna (Irene Adler) and Basil Rathbone (Holmes) in the play Sherlock Holmes *by Ouida Rathbone, 1953, which lasted for only three performances in New York.*

BELOW LEFT:
Poster for the three week try-out of Ouida Rathbone's play in Boston, 'prior to New York, London and World Tour.'

BELOW:
Also in 1953 there was presented The Great Detective, *a ballet at Sadler's Wells, with Kenneth Macmillan as the unnamed but plainly identifiable detective, and Stanley Holden as 'His friend the Doctor.'*

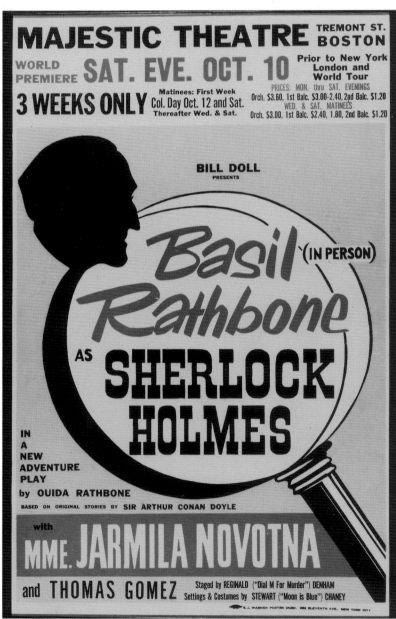

ABOVE:
The Broadway Theater, New York, 1965. The tremendous production costs, including the continuous running of these moving figures, resulted in a loss, despite a year's run.

LEFT:
The well-known misogynist Sherlock Holmes (Fritz Weaver) does not appear unduly distressed to be in the midst of these chorus girls.

OPPOSITE:
The acclaimed TV Holmes and Watson, Jeremy Brett and Edward Hardwicke, took to the London stage in 1988.

ABOVE:
Ron Moody in a persuasive pose as Sherlock Holmes.

RIGHT:
For the purposes of this brochure cover, Moody, like many stage impersonators of Holmes, was saddled with an absurd calabash pipe.

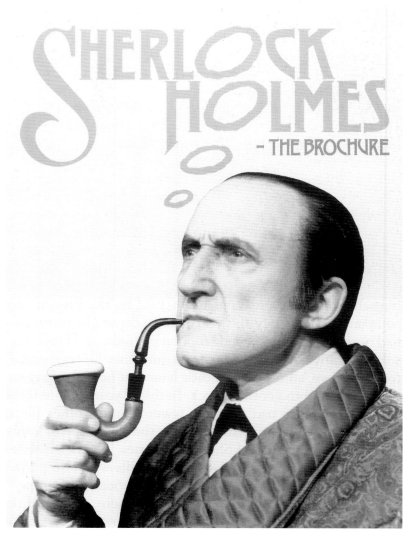

Following the pattern of Eille Norwood, the tremendous publicity gained a decade later by the Granada Television series, with Jeremy Brett as Sherlock Holmes, made it relatively easy for a stage play, *The Secret of Sherlock Holmes* (1988), with Brett and Edward Hardwicke, to run for almost a year in the West End of London with only Holmes and Watson as the characters, and nothing in the way of a plot. While this piece was on at Wyndham's Theater, there also appeared a little further north at the Cambridge Theater *Sherlock Holmes – the Musical*, by Leslie Bricusse, which was another ill-conceived and short-lived venture that sounded at least in part as though it had been prepared with the memories of *Baker Street* in mind.

OPPOSITE:
Eille Norwood's slightly craggy features were in some ways akin to Doyle's original conception of Sherlock Holmes's appearance.

ABOVE:
Norwood and Hubert Willis (Dr Watson, left) confront Percy Standing's frustrated Professor Moriarty, while right: Holmes and Watson confer before burgling the house of the blackmailer Milverton (right).

The suave Clive Brook as Holmes and (above) with H Reeves Smith as Watson in The Return of Sherlock Holmes, *1929.*

TOP RIGHT:
Clive Brook and company on the set of Fox's Sherlock Holmes, *1933.*

BOTTOM RIGHT:
Holmes, in another dressing-gown, Alice (Miriam Jordan) and Billy (Howard Leeds). Sherlock Holmes, *1933.*

Clive Brook had the distinction of being the first actor to appear as the great detective in a 'talkie', *The Return of Sherlock Holmes*. Clive Brook, one of a group of striking-looking men who used to be called 'matinee idols', was numbered amongst those British stage-trained actors whose presence in Hollywood proved invaluable at a time when the primitive sound apparatus of the earliest talkies needed very clear enunciation. (He subsequently starred in numerous sound films, the most famous being *Shanghai Express*, with Marlene Dietrich.)

Paramount had only paid for the right to use the characters of Holmes and Watson, according to the director of the movie, Basil Dean, but presumably the deal included Professor Moriarty and Colonel Moran, since they also appeared. So the story had to be newly concocted; the action took place aboard an ocean liner, and involved Holmes in various disguises, but not much in the way of deductions. Clive Brook was not particularly happy with the direction of the film, for it was Basil Dean's first movie while Brook was already an experienced film actor. Even so, *The Return* was bound to be well received, as the first Sherlock Holmes film with dialogue.

At the time of the introduction of talking pictures the major studios were keen to advertise their respective facilities,

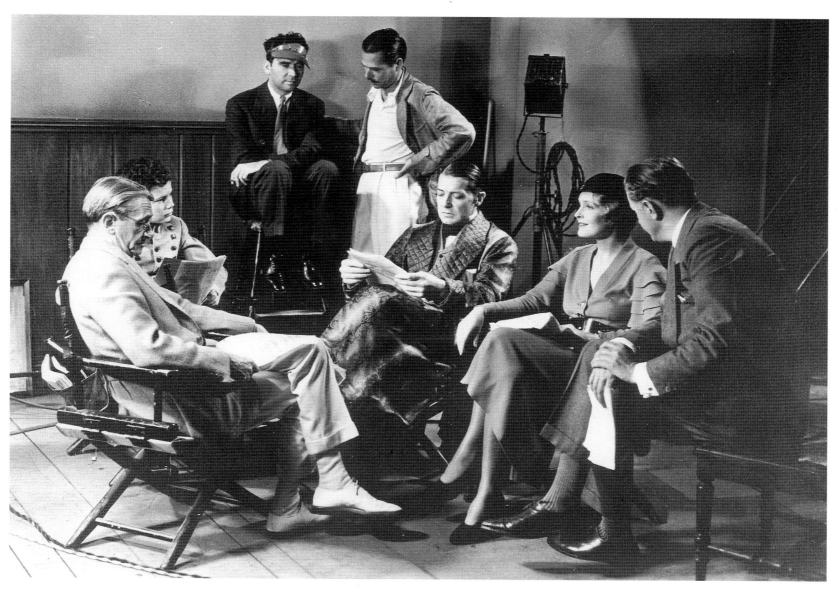

and made omnibus or revue films featuring many of the per-
formers on their payroll in dramatic and comic sketches and
musical turns. The Paramount compilation (released in 1930)
was called *Paramount on Parade*, and included a 'Travesty of
Detective Mysteries' entitled *Murder Will Out*. Clive Brook,
whose long tweed coat must have been still warm from *The
Return*, re-appeared as Holmes, together with William Powell
as Philo Vance, and Warner Oland as Dr Fu Manchu, all
being characters played by those actors in feature films by
Paramount at that time.

The coming of sound to the cinema screen meant that
studios were anxious to remake many of their silent successes
as talkies, and Sherlock Holmes films were no exception. First
after Clive Brook came Arthur Wontner with *The Sleeping
Cardinal* in 1931, followed in the same year by Raymond Massey as Holmes in the only sound film version of *The Speckled
Band*, which also had Lyn Harding as the villain Dr Rylott, the
role he created on the stage when Conan Doyle's play of that
name was first produced. Unfortunately Harding's full-
blooded barnstorming acting was quite unsuited to the
cinema, and simply perpetuated the imbalance that flawed
Doyle's play. In 1932, only a few months after *The Speckled
Band*, there came a dreadfully dull *Hound of the Baskervilles*,
the first sound version, and not to be dwelt upon. As a form of
compensation, one might say, it was closely followed, again
only a few months later, by the second Arthur Wontner film,
The Missing Rembrandt. Indeed, the Sherlock Holmes film
activity in 1932 has never been equaled, with the above-
mentioned three films from British studios, plus another Clive
Brook film from Fox in Hollywood and a fifth from Czechos-
lovakia. Clive Brook's film, just called *Sherlock Holmes*, was
made when he was loaned by Paramount to Fox, and Brook

TOP LEFT:
Dr Fu Manchu (Warner Oland), Sherlock Holmes (Clive Brook), Philo Vance (William Powell) and Sergeant Heath (Eugene Pallette) in Paramount on Parade, *1930.*

BOTTOM LEFT:
Robert Rendel in The Hound of the Baskervilles, *1932.*

RIGHT:
Raymond Massey (Holmes disguised as a workman) in The Speckled Band, *1932.*

ABOVE:
Arthur Wontner sniffs out a clue.

OPPOSITE:
The finest film Sherlock Holmes of the 1930s: Arthur Wontner in The Triumph of Sherlock Holmes, *1935.*

LEFT:
The Hound of the Baskervilles *poses elegantly on the chest of Sir Henry Baskerville (John Stuart), 1932.*

BELOW:
Reginald Owen in A Study in Scarlet, *1933.*

liked neither the loan-out nor the film. He objected to the director, William K Howard, and to the extraordinary script, which had Moriarty escaping from jail and importing American gangsters and international criminals to inflict an unprecedented Chicago-style crime wave on Britain. One has every sympathy with Clive Brook's point of view on this matter, for although William K Howard was a very competent director, able to turn out the required studio product in the form of a very smart, fast-paced crime story, it was just not right for a Sherlock Holmes film, and it is greatly to Brook's credit that he managed to retain some dignity and calm in the film with his customary gentlemanly manner. Dr Watson in this Fox film was played by Reginald Owen, who was almost imperceptible, as he only appeared in two scenes, but perhaps that was just as well, for in the next American-made Holmes film, *A Study in Scarlet* (1933), Reginald Owen was Sherlock Holmes, and he retains that distinction of being the only actor to have portrayed both Holmes and Watson on the screen. The film had nothing to do with the Conan Doyle novel of that name, and was yet another excuse for a lively crime film that just happened to have Sherlock Holmes as one of the characters.

Both of these American films appeared at the same time as a run of five films made in Britain in the 1930s with Arthur Wontner as Sherlock Holmes. At this point it becomes important not to lapse into uncritical admiration, for prior to the Second World War no finer Sherlock Holmes films had been seen in Britain, although in 1939 there was one on the way across the Atlantic that was to change everyone's view of Holmes forever. In Arthur Wontner there was at last an actor who not only looked like the generally accepted image of Sherlock Holmes, but could also act the part convincingly in an

authoritative and dignified way, yet with a relaxed and amiable manner. He appeared in five films which, while mostly based on Conan Doyle stories, were at times very loosely based, and were subject to the box-office needs of all movies to attract people into the cinemas and keep them on their seats. Indeed the first of the Wontner films had proved very successful in the USA, and all of them were shown there.

In the course of a very distinguished stage career, Arthur Wontner had appeared as Sexton Blake, not long before he began his Sherlock Holmes films, and if at times the films seem more Sexton Blake than Sherlock Holmes that was not Wontner's fault. The demands of the 1930s for brisker

detection films with more action and less talk were bound to prevail, and in one instance an American director was employed to pep up the proceedings. The result was *The Sign of Four* (1932), which in a way was an understandable choice, since the climax is an exciting river chase on the Thames, and chases have ever been a staple of action films. The chief faults with the five Wontner films were the 1930s settings, and Wontner's age; while he did not really look his age, his voice betrayed the fact that he was in his sixties. Nonetheless, the five films that he made as Sherlock Holmes stand as a remarkable achievement, and were a portent of even better things to come.

LEFT:
Lady Violet Lumsden (Jane Welsh) consults Sherlock Holmes (Arthur Wontner) and Dr Watson (Ian Fleming) in The Missing Rembrandt, *1932.*

TOP RIGHT:
Holmes and Watson mull over a case in The Triumph of Sherlock Holmes.

BELOW RIGHT:
Holmes menaces a villain with his umbrella, while Watson relieves the crook of his revolver in The Missing Rembrandt.

LEFT:
European film makers repeatedly used the flat cap as a symbol of the Britishness of Sherlock Holmes. Here it is worn with great panache by Hans Albers in Der Mann der Sherlock Holmes war, *1937. The baby-faced Dr Watson was Heinz Rühmann.*

BELOW LEFT:
Herman Speelmans, on the left, as Jimmy Ward alias Sherlock Holmes in Sherlock Holmes – die graue Dame, *1937.*

RIGHT:
Flat caps again for Holmes and Watson (Bruno Güttner and Fritz Odemar) and a leather coat for Holmes, in the 1937 Der Hund von Baskerville.

At the time of Arthur Wontner's last film there appeared in Nazi Germany three more Sherlock Holmes films, and one of these was yet another version of *The Hound of the Baskervilles*, which suggests that the macabre story of a legendary ghostly hound threatening the succession of a branch of the English aristocracy must have held some peculiar fascination for German audiences, or at least German film makers.

Then, in 1939, two important events took place. One was the outbreak of war, but the other, far more important for the purposes of this book, was the production by Twentieth Century-Fox of *The Hound of the Baskervilles*, with Basil Rathbone and Nigel Bruce as Sherlock Holmes and Dr Watson. It was clear from the moment of its release that it was a fine film; over 50 years later it appears to be a great film and probably the unchallenged best Sherlock Holmes film of all. It somehow makes all later versions of the story, and most other Sherlock Holmes films, pale by comparison. A major cause of its success was the inspired casting of the two principals, Holmes

and Watson. The combination of Basil Rathbone and Nigel Bruce was one of those happy partnerships that occur only very rarely in films, or in the entertainment world generally, and it is regrettable that as time went on they were not provided with better productions in which to exercise their talents.

Rathbone began his acting career on the stage in England, before moving to America in the 1920s. As with many stage actors, Hollywood beckoned, and silent pictures led to talking pictures, for which his clear, incisive voice was admirably suited. His dark good looks and tall lithe figure earned him important leading and supporting roles, and he developed an excellent line in villainy. Who can forget his stirring performance as Sir Guy of Gisborne against Errol Flynn's Robin Hood, or his contemptuous Capitan Esteban Pasquale, opposing Tyrone Power's Zorro? Numerous other fine performances spring to mind, but the role for which he is and will ever be remembered is that of Sherlock Holmes. Not only is that because he appeared as Holmes in 14 films in seven years,

LEFT:

The launching of an historic partnership – Nigel Bruce and Basil Rathbone in the first of their 14 films – The Hound of the Baskervilles, *1939.*

ABOVE:

For the first time in talking pictures a Sherlock Holmes film was set in the Victorian period, and in The Hound *Bruce and Rathbone were attired accordingly.*

made over 200 radio broadcasts as Holmes in the same period, made gramophone records of readings of the Holmes stories, and appeared in a television play, but also because from the 1950s onward his Sherlock Holmes films have been shown repeatedly on television, and are still being shown. So for 50 years Rathbone has been the image of Sherlock Holmes in the minds of several generations, and it is small wonder that they think of him as the first Sherlock Holmes in films. There is a telling moment in the 1971 film *They Might Be Giants* when George C. Scott, playing a mentally disturbed person who thinks he is Sherlock Holmes and wanders around dressed in a deerstalker and caped coat, bumps into a policeman who in all seriousness exclaims 'I'm very pleased to meet you, Mr Rathbone!'

Unfortunately this exceptional type of identification of actor with character is disastrous to the actor's career, and after seven years of Holmes, Rathbone found that he was almost unemployable and few major parts were ever given him again. It was a situation that left him extremely

LEFT:
Correct attire again in the second Rathbone/Bruce film The Adventures of Sherlock Holmes, *1939, with Ida Lupino as distressed heroine.*

RIGHT:
The classic image of Holmes, Watson, deerstalker and magnifying-glass, remains delineated in the mind with the features of Rathbone and Bruce.

BELOW:
Sherlock Holmes in Washington, 1942, was an episode in World War Two, and Rathbone's costume and hairstyle underwent a remarkable and unwelcome change.

embittered, but the problem was not unique to Rathbone. After *Sherlock Holmes*, William Gillette did nothing else of consequence, neither did Eille Norwood nor Arthur Wontner, for they all became so closely identified with the character they portrayed that they could not rid themselves of that image.

It is sad too that Rathbone's reputation as Holmes rests on a set of 14 films, of which only the first two are of outstanding merit. *The Hound* is as near perfect as any Sherlock Holmes film is every likely to get, and Fox followed it a mere four months later with *The Adventures of Sherlock Holmes*, in which Moriarty plots to steal the Crown Jewels from the Tower of London, temporarily fooling Holmes with a carefully-laid trail of false clues. Unlike all the previous sound films, and probably all previous Sherlock Holmes films, these two Fox films were elegantly mounted in the correct late-Victorian period, and for the first time on the screen we saw Holmes and Watson attired in the correct costume of the day and traveling in hansom cabs and four-wheelers. In town they

wore the customary top hats, and only on the moors did Holmes don tweeds and deerstalker. The care and expenditure that Fox lavished on these two Holmes films was typical of the first feature productions of a quality Hollywood studio, but Fox did not go in for long series of major films, and allowed their options to lapse.

In 1942 Universal Pictures acquired the film rights, and contracted Rathbone and Bruce to reappear as Holmes and Watson, together with Mary Gordon, also from the Fox films, as the long-suffering landlady Mrs Hudson. The principal characters were the same, but the vehicles in which they were to appear were vastly different. By 1942 the USA were also in the war, and the movie-makers obviously thought it was essential for Britain's greatest detective to be seen performing his war service. Holmes and Watson were consequently pitted against Nazi agents in three preposterous adventures of embarrassing banality. These were followed by two glorious Fox films set in the appropriate era. Universal, however, had put Holmes and Watson in modern dress in

behind Sherlock Holmes in understanding what is going on, so long as we can be just a few steps ahead of Dr Watson. To diminish Watson to the level of comic stooge not only detracted from Rathbone's Holmes, but was unfortunate in that it has been taken as a pattern for many subsequent depictions of Dr Watson, and this is an unhappy side-effect of the 50-year durability of the Rathbone films. Nigel Bruce was aware of the shortcomings of this presentation of Dr Watson, as he acknowledged in his unpublished autobiography: 'Watson, however, in the films, was made much more of a "comic"

character than he ever was in the books. This was with the object of introducing a little light relief. The doctor, as I played him, was a complete stooge for his brilliant friend and one whose intelligence was almost negligible.' When the last film was made in 1946 Rathbone declined to renew his contract with Universal. Nor did he continue with the role on radio, but the damage had been done so far as his career was concerned. From time to time he drifted back into the role, in a television appearance, and in a stage play, *Sherlock Holmes*, written by his wife, which lasted for only three performances

LEFT:
In a brand new deerstalker and caped coat, Peter Cushing came to the cinema screen in the first Sherlock Holmes movie in color. The Hound of the Baskervilles, *1959.*

in New York in 1953.

By this time television was beginning to affect cinema attendances to an ever-increasing degree, and it was not until 1959 that another Sherlock Holmes film was made, this time in England at the Hammer studios, where a run of Frankenstein and Dracula films was being produced. The first color Sherlock Holmes movie starred Peter Cushing, a Hammer Dr Frankenstein, as Holmes, and Christopher Lee, a Hammer Dracula, as Sir Henry Baskerville, for the film was yet another version of *The Hound of the Baskervilles*. As might have been anticipated with a film from Hammer, the horrific aspects of the story were greatly emphasized, with additional nasties like tarantula spiders and a sacrificial stone slab out on the moor. The final film was neither a regular Hammer horror product nor a good Sherlock Holmes film. Three years later Christopher Lee, who should have been cast as Holmes in the Hammer movie, finally achieved the role in a German production called *Sherlock Holmes and the Deadly Necklace*. This curious film, partly based on Conan Doyle's *The Valley of Fear*, had

Thorley Walters as Dr Watson, and while he and Lee delivered their lines in English and were dubbed into German, the remainder of the cast spoke in German. When the film was dubbed into English for distribution in UK and USA, two other actors did the voices for Lee and Walters, much to Lee's indignation. The chief value of the film was to make one wish to see how Christopher Lee would fare as Holmes in a better production.

The next movie to be made, also in color, was *A Study in Terror* (1965), from an original script by Donald and Derek Ford. It was the first film to depict Sherlock Holmes dealing with the real-life unsolved mystery of the Jack the Ripper killings, which took place in London in 1888. It is an idea that has since been adopted by a further film and several novels, but *A Study in Terror* is by far the best version of the concept, and remains one of the few outstanding post-Rathbone films of merit. For once the parts of the principals were written with the understanding that Holmes and Watson were loyal companions, and the actors concerned, John Neville and Donald

SHERLOCK HOLMES' MOST TERRIFYING ADVENTURE!

PETER CUSHING
as SHERLOCK HOLMES

ANDRE MORELL
as Dr. Watson

CHRISTOPHER LEE
as Sir Henry Baskerville

MARLA LANDI

DAVID OXLEY

the HOUND of the Baskervilles

TECHNICOLOR

Based on the novel by Sir Arthur Conan Doyle

·A·

Produced by ANTHONY HINDS
Directed by TERENCE FISHER
Executive Producer MICHAEL CARRERAS
Associate Producer ANTHONY NELSON KEYS
Screenplay by PETER BRYAN

A HAMMER FILM PRODUCTION

UNITED ARTISTS

ABOVE:
*Hammer ('the House of Horror')
found it difficult to exploit the
horrific elements of the novel while
remaining within the framework of
the story. The result was not very
successful.*

LEFT:
*At a disadvantage in following the
lengthy Rathbone exposure as
Holmes, Peter Cushing proved to be
rather lightweight in both stature
and voice.*

RIGHT:
*In The Hound Cushing had the
support of an excellent Dr Watson
(Andre Morell), seen here at
Baskerville Hall with the
Barrymores, played by John le
Mesurier and Helen Goss.*

LEFT & ABOVE:
Christopher Lee, in Sherlock Holmes und das Halsband des Todes, *1962, suffered from the European desire to clad Holmes in the most conspicuous check garments obtainable.*

RIGHT:
The European publicity for the Hammer Hound *was if anything a little more striking than the British.*

LES ARTISTES ASSOCIÉS S.A.B. *présentent*

PETER CUSHING

ANDRE MORELL

CHRISTOPHER LEE

et MARLA LANDI

le CHIEN des BASKERVILLE

"THE HOUND OF THE BASKERVILLES"

TECHNICOLOR

DE HOND VAN BASKERVILLE

D'APRES LE ROMAN DE SIR ARTHUR CONAN DOYLE · MISE en SCÈNE: TERENCE FISHER · PRODUIT PAR ANTHONY HINDS · SCÉNARIO DE PETER BRYAN · PRODUCTEUR EXECUTIF: MICHAEL CARRERAS · UNE PRODUCTION HAMMER FILM

ABOVE:
More conventional Victorian attire in the excellent A Study in Terror, *1965, with Frank Findlay (Inspector Lestrade), John Neville (Holmes) and Donald Houston (Watson).*

RIGHT:
American publicity for the film seems not to have taken it entirely seriously.

BELOW:
Adrian Conan Doyle, son of the author, visited the set while A Study in Terror *was in production.*

MICHAEL KLINGER & TONY TENSER present

**SPELL IT WITH EXCITEMENT
—THE NAME IS...
SHERLOCK HOLMES**

A STUDY IN TERROR x

IN EASTMAN COLOUR

STARRING

JOHN NEVILLE · DONALD HOUSTON · JOHN FRASER
ANTHONY QUAYLE · BARBARA WINDSOR

SPECIAL GUEST STAR   GUEST STARS

ROBERT MORLEY · GEORGIA BROWN · BARRY JONES · CECIL PARKER

EXECUTIVE PRODUCER   PRODUCED BY   DIRECTED BY
HERMAN COHEN · HENRY E. LESTER · JAMES HILL   A COMPTON-SIR NIGEL FILMS PRODUCTION

A COMPTON RELEASE

Until Nov. 24th _Leicester Square_ THEATRE PHONE WHI. 5252
NORTH LONDON from NOVEMBER 28th
SOUTH LONDON from DECEMBER 5th

*British publicity did not disclose that the film had to do with Jack
the Ripper, but confined itself to the inherent drama of a Holmes story.
As no star names were involved, it was frequently heralded as
'Sherlock Holmes in A Study in Terror'.*

LEFT:
John Neville presented a younger, more virile Holmes than many that have appeared on the screen. At the time the film was being made he was also director of the Nottingham Playhouse, and flew almost daily between Nottingham and Shepperton studios to accomplish both jobs.

RIGHT:
Costume was selected most conscientiously for A Study in Terror, and both Holmes and Watson wore customary evening dress at the appropriate times, even though they did have to defend themselves in the East End of London.

Houston, made excellent use of the opportunities given them by a good script, which conveyed the horrors of the Ripper killings without resorting to explicit illustrations.

From the all-time high of five movies in one year (1932), the rate of making Sherlock Holmes cinema films had slowed right down to about one film every five years, and it was 1970 before Billy Wilder's much-vaunted *The Private Life of Sherlock Holmes* finally reached the screen. Wilder, as someone observed, had come to mock and stayed to revere, and while several important episodes were drastically cut by the Mirisch Corporation before the film was released, it was still a remarkably affectionate and entertaining film, lavishly produced and beautifully filmed, and certainly the costliest Sherlock Holmes film ever made. Sadly it was not a box office success, and would probably have been understood and enjoyed more had the picture not been so heavily edited. Robert Stephens gave an interesting performance of the vulnerable Sherlock Holmes that Billy Wilder wanted to convey, but while Stephens has a distinctive voice that is fine for many parts he has played, it is not right for Holmes. Colin Blakely, an other-

In The Private Life of Sherlock Holmes, *1970, Dr Watson (Colin Blakely) is shocked to see a female kissing Holmes (Robert Stephens).*

LEFT:
Watson is even more shocked when they travel to Scotland masquerading as man and wife.

TOP RIGHT:
Tamara Toumanova, Robert Stephens and Clive Revill prepare for a scene at the ballet; Colin Blakely is not yet in costume.

BOTTOM RIGHT:
Watson takes a letter to Holmes in his bath, to the disapproval of Mrs Hudson (Irene Handl).

LEFT:
Nicol Williamson, a neurotic Sherlock Holmes in The Seven-Per-Cent Solution, *1976.*

TOP RIGHT:
Holmes (Nicol Williamson) and Watson (Robert Duvall), with a bloodhound used in an episode culled from the novel The Sign of Four.

BOTTOM RIGHT:
Watson (Robert Duvall) and Sigmund Freud (Alan Arkin) rescue Holmes from an arena of over-excited performing horses.

wise excellent actor, appeared to suffer from being directed by Wilder in some scenes as if he were Jack Lemmon, all in an eager frenzy.

Another five or six years elapsed before Sherlock Holmes was brought to the screen again, in a dramatization by Nicholas Meyer of his own novel *The Seven-Per-Cent Solution* (1976). The title is an allusion to Holmes's one-time reliance on drugs when, in the story *The Sign of Four*, Watson related with regret how he observed Holmes's addiction. 'Which is it today,' asks Watson, 'morphine or cocaine?' 'Cocaine,' replies Holmes, 'a seven-per-cent solution.' The film depicts Watson's determined endeavors to get Holmes to Vienna, where the celebrated Dr Sigmund Freud eventually effects a cure, but Holmes, Watson and Freud become involved in an adventure concerning another of Freud's patients, and the climax of the film is a rather absurd swordfight between Holmes and the principal villain on the carriage roofs of a fast-moving train, a film cliché stemming from silent picture days. Most of the characters were written and cast against type, which is a

foolish approach to a Sherlock Holmes film, and it resulted in a great waste of talent, with which the cast was bulging. Nicol Williamson was a nervously agitated Holmes, not at all convincing even when cured by Freud, while the American Robert Duvall as Watson delivered such stiff and strangulated English that audiences must have felt as uncomfortable as he sounded. The outstanding performances in the film were by Alan Arkin as Freud, and a superb cameo from Laurence Olivier as a timid Professor Moriarty, a former maths tutor to Holmes, who cringes as he complains about Holmes's incessant and mistaken persecution of him as the Napoleon of Crime. The overall impression of the extravagantly produced and photographed film was one of regrettable waste, and any solution of a crime that Holmes might have achieved was barely seven per cent effective.

In *Murder by Decree* (1980), made in England by a Canadian company, Sherlock Holmes again encountered Jack the Ripper, and in doing so he revealed a massive Establishment cover-up to protect the Royal Family. Holmes,

LEFT & BELOW:
The latest Holmes and Watson team of any stature on the cinema screen was the combination of two excellent actors, Christopher Plummer and James Mason, in Murder By Decree, 1980.

energetically played by Christopher Plummer, was supported by the courageous Watson of James Mason, and Inspector Lestrade, again played by Frank Finlay (previously Lestrade in the Holmes/Ripper film *A Study in Terror*), was handicapped by the presence of Inspector Foxborough (David Hemmings), a secret collaborator with the anarchist movement. Holmes's investigations purported 'to show a disintegrating Victorian society, with a decadent monarchy, an establishment corrupted by freemasonry and a vigorous and no less corrupt radical anarchist movement.' The story becomes so complicated that at the end, and really for the benefit of the audience, Sherlock Holmes has a long scene with the Prime Minister Lord Salisbury and the Home Secretary, in the unlikely setting of a masonic temple, recapitulating the plot to make it all clear. A better script could have done that from the outset, and that is a great pity, because the settings were splendid and the treatment of the Ripper killings skilfully horrific. One critic rightly called it the bloodiest Holmes film yet.

The ever-developing trend towards more violence and distasteful forms of horror in the cinema has gone hand-in-hand with an increasing number of movies aimed at the younger cinema audiences of today, and pre-eminent among film-makers catering for this younger market has been Steven

LEFT:
Back to flashy dressing-gowns for both Holmes and Watson (Radovan Lukavsky and Vaclav Voska) in the Czech film Touka Sherlocka Holmese, *1971.*

ABOVE & RIGHT:
Nicholas Rowe and Alan Cox as the embryonic Holmes and Watson in Young Sherlock Holmes and the Pyramid of Fear, *1986.*

Spielberg, with money-spinners like *ET, Indiana Jones* and *Back to the Future.* In 1986 he took up the idea, first used by Granada with their TV serial *Young Sherlock* in 1982, of depicting the schooldays of Sherlock Holmes and showing him antagonizing nearly everybody with his precocious deductions. This treatment began well enough, with the young Holmes demonstrating his powers of observation and reasoning, and gradually becoming embroiled in a real-life mystery. Then, as is customary at about the half-way mark in most Spielberg films, the obsession with bizarre special effects took over, and the film degenerated into yet another Spielberg fantasy. The title *Young Sherlock Holmes and the Pyramid of Fear* was plainly emulative of the various *Indiana Jones* film titles, and presumably leaves the door ajar for a sequel or two, against which there is always the problem that young actors do not remain young. The title also refers to the set-piece climax in a huge Egyptian pyramid that just happens to have been built unnoticed, inside a London dockland warehouse; it is so implausible that it is clearly a conceit of Spielberg's and has nothing to do with a Conan Doyle fantasy.

CHAPTER 4
THE GREAT IMPERSONATORS ON TELEVISION

MISSING OUT ON the first stage presentation, America has been first with Sherlock Holmes in almost every other branch of entertainment and show business; first on film, first on radio, and in 1937 the first on television, when as part of an evening of experimental television broadcast from Radio City, New York, the NBC company presented a dramatization of *The Three Garridebs*, a Conan Doyle short story first published in 1924. The 30 minute program was broadcast live, as was all early television, and was innovative in using filmed inserts of exterior scenes to link the live interior scenes. The choice of story was understandable, for in *The Three Garridebs*, Sherlock Holmes unmasks an American, John Garrideb, Counsellor-at-Law, as none other than Killer Evans from Chicago, and the piece only needed two interior scenes to make it feasible for live transmission. Louis Hector, as Sherlock Holmes, was no stranger to the role, having already appeared in a series of 29 radio broadcasts in the 1934-35 season; William Podmore was Dr Watson.

The notion of presenting any other Sherlock Holmes adventures on television cannot have been either attractive or particularly practical, and nothing further was seen until television was resumed after the war, when in 1951 *The Mazarin Stone* was transmitted by the BBC, with Andrew Osborn as Holmes and Philip King as Watson. The friendly reception of this adaptation may have persuaded the BBC to produce a series of six weekly adventures on television, with Alan Wheatley, a regular radio and film character actor, as Sherlock Holmes. The stories were lovingly produced by Ian Atkins and dramatized by Caroline Lejeune, an esteemed British film critic but inexperienced in writing for television. To be fair, television productions were still at an experimental stage in 1951, and while the settings and performances were good, the series lacked dramatic tension and real mystery, elements not always easy to achieve with live transmissions.

However, it did establish the standard of faithfulness to the settings of the original stories which has, with rare exceptions, been followed ever since in television adaptations.

A unique television broadcast in 1953 was the CBS presentation of *The Adventure of the Black Baronet*. Conan Doyle's son Adrian, in collaboration with the famous detective story writer John Dickson Carr, had written a series

LEFT:
Louis Hector, the first Holmes on television.

TOP RIGHT:
John Gielgud (Holmes) and Ralph Richardson (Watson) recorded a series of radio broadcasts in 1954.

BOTTOM RIGHT:
Carleton Hobbes and Norman Shelley were Holmes and Watson on BBC radio for 15 years. Here they are seen in costume in the replica room in the Sherlock Holmes pub in 1959.

of 12 new short stories now known as *The Exploits of Sherlock Holmes*, and *The Black Baronet* was televized in May 1953 to coincide with the first publication of that story in *Colliers* magazine. It was broadcast from New York in the immensely popular CBS *Suspense* mystery series of half-hour plays, and was distinguished by having Basil Rathbone as Sherlock Holmes. Nigel Bruce was prevented by poor health from joining Rathbone in New York to play Watson once more, and Martyn Green filled his place. The program was also regarded as useful publicity for a proposed stage play *Sherlock*

OPPOSITE:
*Sherlock Holmes (Alan Wheatley)
reads from the agony column of*
The Times *to Dr Watson
(Raymond Francis) in* The Red
Headed League.

ABOVE:
The Red Headed League *was an
adventure in the first television
Sherlock Holmes series by the BBC
in 1951. Waiting to ambush the
bank robbers are Inspector Lestrade
(Bill Owen), Mr Merryweather
(Arthur Goulett), Holmes and
Watson.*

LEFT:
*Alan Wheatley felt that his career
had been blighted by appearing in a
Sherlock Holmes series.*

Holmes, written by Rathbone's wife, which was then in pre-paration.

The New Adventures of Sherlock Holmes were, as the title of the series suggests, mostly new, although some were adaptations, or near misses, of Conan Doyle stories. The series was the brain-child of the producer Sheldon Reynolds and totaled 39 episodes, running for almost a year from October 1954 on NBC Television. It was filmed in France for reasons of economy, and had Ronald Howard as a youthful-looking Sherlock Holmes and Howard Marion Crawford as Dr Watson. The films, each 27 minutes long, began with *The Case of the Cunningham Heritage*, the first half of which is spent in depicting the very first meeting of Holmes and Watson in St Bartholemew's Hospital, a meeting that has never otherwise been shown on the screen. *The New Adventures* were written by a number of expatriate Hollywood writers, and ranged from interesting and adequate dramas, through standard television fodder to the downright silly. In *The Texas Cowgirl*, for example, a Red Indian Chief in full dress, a fugitive from a traveling Wild West show, erected a tepee inside the Baker Street consulting room; in *The Baker Street Nurse-maids* the two companions were, as the title infers, landed with baby-minding, while in *The Baker Street Bachelors* they were involved in seeking wives at a marriage bureau in the course of investigating a blackmail case. Thankfully not many of the

ABOVE:
Dr Watson (Nigel Stock) faces the Holmes brothers, Mycroft (Derek Francis) and Sherlock (Douglas Wilmer), in The Bruce Partington Plans, *1965.*

RIGHT:
Douglas Wilmer at work in Sherlock Holmes's 'chemistry corner.'

OPPOSITE:
Wilmer's appearance was occasionally reminiscent of Basil Rathbone, and his performances, with Nigel Stock as Watson, were undervalued at the time.

episodes were as pathetic and embarrassing as these, but such examples made it hard to take very seriously such a variable and inconsistent series. It has survived to be repeated often on American television, but has never been shown in Britain.

In 1951 Alan Wheatley had discovered the detrimental effect that playing Holmes had on his career: he had no further roles of importance other than on radio. In 1955 Ronald Howard experienced much the same sort of thing. After the Wheatley series on BBC any further notions of another Holmes series were quashed for some years by the great success on Independent Television of a series featuring a Victorian detective named Sergeant Cork.

In a fascinating series called simply *Detective*, the BBC in 1964 presented each week a different fictional detective, some well-known, others not, in a single adventure. The series provided a useful number of pilot programs for ideas that later became various series. On 18 May *The Speckled Band* was shown with Douglas Wilmer as Sherlock Holmes and Nigel Stock as Dr Watson, and was evidently very favorably

regarded. The following year a series of 12 adventures with these two actors was heralded by the BBC as 'the first full-dress nation-wide series featuring Sherlock Holmes,' a disgraceful dismissal of the BBC's own 1951 series. It is true that the new series was better, as being made on film it could not fail to be, but the Conan Doyle stories concerned were all adapted to a 50-minute length, which was too long and necessitated padding in nearly every episode. Apart from that, the adaptations were the work of a team of television writers supervised by the overall script editor Anthony Read. Any shortcomings in the series were doubtless due to the speed with which these episodes, like many other television series, were made.

Many years afterwards, Douglas Wilmer, clearly a devotee of the stories and not merely an actor employed for a job, revealed the extent to which he had been involved in amending the scripts and generally insisting on some reasonable standards of intelligibility and presentation in the series. He was very conscious of the sheer weight of responsibility of

playing such a famous and familiar character in such well-loved stories: 'I was directed in 13 plays by eight directors. Before undertaking the series at all I had stipulated a maximum of three, as I was concerned, with good reason as it turned out, with problems of over-all continuity and consistency of style.'

Three years later, in 1968, the BBC presented a further series of 15 Conan Doyle stories, all different from the previous series, and this time in color. Nigel Stock was still Dr Watson, but Douglas Wilmer had determined not to step on the treadmill again: 'When I was offered the second series, it was with rehearsals cut down from 14 days to ten for "reasons of economy". Naturally I refused,' stated Wilmer. 'There being some unwisdom at the helm, they persisted in this stipulation – I wouldn't have done it anyway, not again, and they approached two or three actors of repute who also declined. Poor Peter Cushing unwisely accepted. He was, of course, unaware of the circumstances into which he was to find himself and when he did, coupled with the insecurity of a beggarly ten

days rehearsal, the results were not good.'

The choice of Peter Cushing became significant when the aspects of horror and violence that pervaded the series were seen, and that was quite deliberate, as the clumsy publicity of the BBC warned: 'What is new in this series is the basic approach – a daring realization of the lurking horror and callous savagery of Victorian crime, especially sexual crime. Here is the re-creation of the half-world of brutal males and the furtive innocents they dominate; of evil-hearted servants scheming and embracing below stairs; of murder, mayhem and the macabre . . .' The series as a whole betrayed great haste in production, one episode being transmitted before final editing had been completed. That haste plainly affected Peter Cushing's performances in the leading role. Douglas Wilmer proved to be quite right in his observations, and was wise to keep out of it, leaving his own series as something in which he can still take some pride.

In addition to being omniscient, Sherlock Holmes certainly appeared to be omnipresent when he appeared in two

LEFT:
Peter Cushing took over the role of Sherlock Holmes on BBC television in 1968; Nigel Stock stayed on as Watson.

RIGHT:
Cushing and Stock appeared in 15 adaptations of the Conan Doyle stories in 1968.

BELOW:
The Hound of the Baskervilles *was transmitted in two parts; this was Cushing's second time in the story.*

RIGHT:
Vasily Livanov and Vitaly Solomin as Holmes and Watson in a Russian TV series of 1969.

BELOW:
Nando Gazzolo (far left) as Holmes, seated in Italian TV's idea of Baskerville Hall, 1968.

adventures on RAI Television in Italy in 1968, and even penetrated the Iron Curtain in 1969, in several stories made for Russian television. In France in 1974 Rolf Becker played Holmes in *Monsieur Sherlock Holmes*, based on *The Sign of Four*, and this was also shown on Swedish television.

Stewart Granger, one of the last British film stars to emigrate to Hollywood, appeared in numerous American films and television productions, and in 1972 played Sherlock Holmes in a color film of *The Hound of the Baskervilles*, made by Universal for ABC Television as part of a projected series

of famous detectives. The series never got past the first two films (*Nick Carter* was the second), and this dull and uninspired version of *The Hound* cannot have helped the future of the series at all. Granger's casual, relaxed style of acting was unsuited to the part of Holmes, and he has never completely lost the aura of glamour that attached to him in his younger days.

'Look who's next in line for the deerstalker' trumpeted one newspaper headline when the casting of Roger Moore as Sherlock Holmes became known in 1976. The newspaper

ABOVE:
Dr Watson and the Darkwater
Hall Mystery, *written by Kingsley
Amis for BBC television in 1974,
featured Watson (Edward Fox)
without Holmes.*

RIGHT:
*Bernard Fox and Stewart Granger
in yet another version of* The
Hound of the Baskervilles.

LEFT:
The stars of Sherlock Holmes in
New York: *John Huston, Charlotte
Rampling, Patrick MacNee and
Roger Moore.*

RIGHT:
*Why property managers repeatedly
saddle actors playing Holmes with
an enormous and impractical
calabash pipe is a continuing
mystery. Here the strain is being
taken by Roger Moore.*

went on, predictably, to present a little selection of previous screen Holmeses and then reflected on Moore's career to date. On British television Roger Moore had established himself as a handsome hero in the *Ivanhoe* series, and later in the long-running and enormously popular series *The Saint*, following which he succeeded Sean Connery as James Bond in the cinema. Not surprisingly a number of pieces in the Press scoffed at the idea of Bond becoming Holmes, but were remarkably silent when it actually happened, and worst fears were not realized. *Sherlock Holmes in New York* was, like *The Seven-Per-Cent Solution*, crammed with talent, but made rather better use of it. Besides the urbane Patrick MacNee as Dr Watson, the film had John Huston as Moriarty, Charlotte Rampling as Irene Adler (the only woman for whom Holmes is reputed to have felt any affection), Gig Young, Signe Hasso and Jackie Coogan. The direction could have been better suited to the personalities of the leading players, who nevertheless did a passable job aided by an original and clever script that had Holmes drawn to New York by Moriarty's

machinations in a plot that included a gold robbery and the kidnapping of the alleged son of Adler and Holmes. The TV film was a joint production of NBC Television and Twentieth Century-Fox.

The BBC's apparent monopoly of Sherlock Holmes on television in Britain was eventually broken in 1977 when Harlech Television presented a 30-minute adaptation of the short story *Silver Blaze*, with Christopher Plummer as Holmes, and Thorley Walters giving his second performance as Watson (the first was in Christopher Lee's German film). For all the expenditure incurred in mounting the piece, it was a mild disappointment, since Plummer, a very interesting portrayer of the role, was not helped by either direction or editing. After this minor production television screens were free of new Sherlock Holmes pieces for some time, although the numerous feature films continued to be recycled ad nauseam, until in 1982 there came an unprecedented outbreak of activity on both the BBC and independent television channels, each appearing to vie with the other in announcing, months in

Full front cover treatment for Sherlock Holmes on the two leading British TV magazines.

RIGHT:
Christopher Plummer's first portrayal of Holmes was in Silver Blaze *on TV in 1977. Thorley Walters was Watson.*

advance, new serials and series, all clouded by the vexed issue of copyright differences between Britain and America. In Britain and Europe Conan Doyle's copyright expired in 1980, 50 years after his death, but in America the copyright exists for 75 years, and since Doyle's only surviving daughter had sold the rights to an American company, there were obvious problems in any British productions being sold to the USA.

Undeterred, the BBC produced yet another version of *The Hound of the Baskervilles*, which it announced as 'the new Sunday family serial'. It was shown in four episodes, and gave

the impression of being perversely cast against type so as to ridicule the cult of Sherlock Holmes. Tom Baker's high-speed overacting as Holmes and Terence Rigby's woefully out-of-depth Watson contributed to a deplorable presentation. The week after it concluded, Granada Television's serial *Young Sherlock*, also shown on Sunday evening, began an eight-week run, and proved a welcome and enjoyable concept which quickly obliterated the memory of the preceding *Hound*. The premise was that of a young Sherlock Holmes, home from school to find his parents have fled abroad because of his

LEFT:
Terence Rigby (Watson) and Tom Baker (Holmes) in the BBC serial of The Hound of the Baskervilles, *1982.*

BELOW LEFT:
Ronald Fraser and Hugh Fraser in Murder on the Bluebell Line, *a BBC drama documentary about the Piltdown hoax, 1987.*

BELOW RIGHT:
Guy Henry as Young Sherlock, *1982.*

father's bankruptcy, so young Sherlock has to lodge in the somewhat Dickensian household of his uncle. Before long there is a corpse, and the youngster's investigations, at times frustrated by family constraints and thwarted by what turn out to be genuine evil participants, eventually lead him to a successful rescue of Queen Victoria herself. Guy Henry was excellent in the title role, and it is not altogether surprising that this notion of schoolday exploits of the great detective was later taken up on an altogether grander scale.

Youngsters in abundance occupied the next television

*The stylish and always watchable
actor Ian Richardson in an
excellent Baker Street setting.*

*Ian Richardson (Holmes) and
Donald Churchill (Watson) in* The
Hound of the Baskervilles, *1983.*

series when the BBC's *The Baker Street Boys* (1983) was devoted to the activities of the Baker Street Irregulars, the group
of street urchins who were Sherlock Holmes's eyes and ears in
the less salubrious parts of London. This happy idea showed
the boys (and of course in this egalitarian age, two girls as well)
solving a few mysteries on their own, or nearly on their own,
while Holmes is preoccupied with weightier matters. The
series won the writer Anthony Read, former script editor of
the Wilmer series, a well-earned award for an original chil-
drens' television series.

Meanwhile in America in 1983 the two TV films made
by the Lorindy company as a result of their deal with Jean
Conan Doyle, were shown. They were both full-length versions of two of the long stories, *The Sign of Four* and *The
Hound of the Baskervilles*. They were filmed in England at the
Shepperton studios, and featured Ian Richardson as Sherlock
Holmes, as well as two substantial casts of British character
actors. *The Sign of Four* was an exceedingly enjoyable production, with a beautifully restrained performance by Richardson. In fact both Holmes and Watson (David Healy) were very

human and believable and the whole production reflected great credit on Lorindy. *The Hound*, on the other hand, was not as impressive, even though much of the production seemed to have been copied from the 1939 Rathbone *Hound*. Dr Watson was now played by Donald Churchill instead of David Healy, a decidedly inferior substitution, and there were quite unnecessary additions to the story such as a silly fortune-telling scene in a gipsy camp, and the brutal killing of Laura Lyons, who is only an incidental character in the novel. It seemed as though there was a determination to hype up the production with as much gratuitous violence and similar distractions simply because *The Hound* has been filmed so many times before, and this one had to be different. The benefits of the film were the performances of Richardson, and of Denholm Elliott as Dr Mortimer; their acting almost made up for a generally weak film.

These two Richardson films were not shown on British television until the end of 1988, by which time there had been four years in which the Granada Television series of adaptations of the stories had been transmitted and repeated, so that British television audiences, at least, had been conditioned to the impersonation of Jeremy Brett as Sherlock Holmes in no fewer than *22* adventures before Richardson was seen, and two of these were the same stories as the Richardson films. The conflict between the two projects for major television productions was by no means a straight-

RIGHT:
Where else could this Sherlock Holmes be but in London? Jeremy Brett at Westminster, 1984.

BELOW:
Jeremy Brett, Jenny Seagrove and Edward Hardwicke (Watson) in The Sign of Four, *1987.*

forward coincidence of planning, for the rights to all the Holmes stories published after 1906 are still controlled in America, and were the subject of a widely reported major deal between the Lorindy company and Conan Doyle's daughter Jean. The effect of this was that Granada Television's series would be denied an American market, and lengthy litigation followed, for Granada had invested heavily in its ambitious program, even to the extent of building a semi-permanent Baker Street outdoor set alongside the famous Coronation Street set at the Granada Manchester studios.

The matter was eventually settled out of court, with Granada making payment to Lorindy so that the Granada series can be shown in America, while Lorindy appear to have abandoned plans for any further productions at present. From the public's point of view it seems a satisfactory arrangement, for the care and accuracy of settings and presentation achieved by the Granada team have been second to none. As always, the short stories have been adopted to a uniform 50 minute length, to suit television programing schedules, whereas the stories themselves vary quite a lot both in length and in the amount of performable drama they contain. It is a problem that confronts all dramatists who tackle the Sherlock Holmes canon, and in the case of the Granada series it has on the whole been handled very well, with short additional side issues inserted very judiciously where necessary.

The difficulty with the Granada series, in the opinion of the present writer, has been in attempting to make the adaptations too faithful to the original stories. What seems to have been overlooked is the fundamental change between reading the stories and seeing them dramatized. The reader sees everything through the eyes of Dr Watson, who acts as a buffer between the reader and the remarkable, idiosyncratic, unpredictable, highly knowledgeable, highly intelligent, single-minded and unemotional character Sherlock Holmes. In a dramatization, whether on the stage or screen, the softening effect of Watson's account of this character is lost. The reader is assured by Watson that in spite of his attitudes and

ABOVE:
The first Dr Watson with Jeremy Brett's Holmes was David Burke.

RIGHT:
In The Final Problem *Brett's Holmes was pitted against the Professor Moriarty of Eric Porter.*

OPPOSITE:
The celebrated death struggle scenes were, for the first time, actually filmed at the Reichenbach Falls in Switzerland.

mannerisms, Holmes is really a deeply sensitive and caring person. In the drama, however, we are faced with Holmes direct, without the benefit of this filter, and it seems that in the Granada series little or no account has been taken of this; the viewer is presented with a version of Holmes that at times is very unattractive.

The demands of television production schedules are such that to expect a consistent standard of adaptation and direction throughout a long series, written and directed by a team of writers and directors, is to hope for too much, and the Granada series fluctuated accordingly. For Jeremy Brett to cope with all these disadvantages, and to follow all the

preceding Holmeses, many of whom keep reappearing on television, was an impossible task. Adverse critical reviews of the series may not have taken this into account, and one is frequently in the position of liking particular episodes but not liking Brett's Holmes; and the low spots in the series only seemed to aggravate this reaction. Brett's over-acting and shouting, at times ranting, was not in character, and in *The Bruce-Partington Plans*, for example, his bawling for Mrs Hudson, and later telling her to 'Disappear!' was not what one has come to expect from someone whom Watson describes as having remarkable gentleness and courtesy when dealing with women, even domestics. Nevertheless, it must be acknow-

ABOVE:
Peter Cushing's final appearance as Sherlock Holmes was in The Masks of Death, *1984.*

LEFT:
Cushing's companion in this adventure was the trusty John Mills as Dr Watson.

TOP RIGHT:
Peter Cushing, ever a master of 'pipe business' portrayed an ageing Holmes very skilfully.

BOTTOM RIGHT:
Yet to be shown at the time of writing, Patrick MacNee (Watson), Morgan Fairchild (Irene Adler) and Christopher Lee (Holmes) in Sherlock Holmes and the Leading Lady.

ledged that the Granada series is a major landmark in the whole history of Sherlock Holmes dramatizations, and it will be interesting to see whether the Granada team will have the financial backing, to say nothing of the ingenuity, to conclude the first ever complete set of TV dramatizations of the 60 Conan Doyle stories.

In between the first and second sets of the Granada TV *Adventures of Sherlock Holmes* came a TV film *Sherlock Holmes and the Masks of Death*, in which a rather elderly Holmes and Watson, played by an equally elderly Peter Cushing and John Mills, uncovered and thwarted a dastardly plot by the wicked Germans to leak poison gas into the homes of Londoners by way of the domestic gas supply. This sounds more outlandish than it actually appeared on the screen, and the script caught the right mixture of dark crimes and quiet good-natured humor that is so difficult to achieve, and without which Sherlock Holmes dramatizations are seldom very satisfying. The wicked Germans divert the famous detective to a sealed-room mystery in Buckinghamshire, where one of the guests at the country house turns out to be Irene Adler. In time Holmes

sees through the ruse and returns to solve the real mystery. It was not one of the best Holmes film, but nor was it one to be ashamed of as Peter Cushing's final performance in the role of Holmes.

It may be that further convulsions on television embroiling the great detective are yet to be seen and experienced. The following extracts from an article by Charles Bremner in New York explain the position:

'If you are the kind of person who knows who dunnit while Poirot or Columbo are still faltering after false leads, take heart. A Californian television company has created a device that will let you tell the bumbling detective, via a keypad, what his next step should be. If enough viewers agree with you, the sleuth will follow your advice.

'Called *Sherlock Phones*, the detective show is one of the more ambitious of a plethora of experiments which let viewers take control of their television screens . . . In the early 1980s several American companies tried and failed to entice viewers with crude attempts at two-way television . . . Now, with fiber optics, and computers and multi-channel cable installed in over half of America's homes, entrepreneurs and advertisers of *Sherlock Phones*, devised by Laser Arts Interactive of Los Angeles, the story is filmed with numerous variations. At the moment the studio broadcasts the action chosen by the majority of viewers, but in future, the program may be tailored to the individual, just as in a computer game.

'While enthusiasts speak of new horizons, sceptics doubt if the couch potato has any taste for getting involved in the direction and casting of a favorite program. "Most of the time, what the individual wants to do is sit back and relax," Russel Newman, a television expert told the New York Times.'

CHAPTER 5
THE GREAT IMPOSTORS

THE FAMOUS AMERICAN humorist H L Mencken once wrote that the final test of fame is to have a crazy person imagine he is you. Of course it is possible to make fun of someone completely unknown, but nobody else will understand it, and parodies, satires, burlesques, skits, take-offs, send-ups, or whatever you choose to call them, are only successful if the object of that humor is well enough known to the audience to be instantly recognized and understood. The massive testimony to the widespread knowledge and popularity of Sherlock Holmes is found not only in the repeated publications of the stories and all the dramatizations and discussions of the same, but also, and especially, in the countless occasions when he has been used for comic purposes.

This seems to have begun even when the Holmes short stories were appearing in *The Strand Magazine* in 1893, when the very first British comic strip *The Adventures of Chubb-Lock Homes* appeared in *Comic Cuts*. (In the second instalment a week later the artist accidentally used the name Sherlock Holmes in the heading, but the mistake was never repeated). Later the same year Holmes and Watson were parodied on the stage in *Under the Clock*, as described in Chapter 2. This piece cannot have remained unknown to Conan Doyle, although no reference was ever made to it by him. Similarly he must certainly have been aware of the burlesque *Sheerluck Jones* (1901), which was a travesty of the William Gillette play then appearing at the Lyceum Theater in London. The Charles Frohman organization, responsible for the business management of the Gillette play throughout the world, were actively protecting their business interests by hunting down every unauthorized Sherlock Holmes dramatization and obtaining legal sanctions to prevent anyone else benefiting from the Gillette play's great success. Numerous touring companies were either forced to include in their advertising a disclaimer of any connection with the Lyceum production, or were prevented from using the title *Sherlock Holmes*.

The appearance of *Sheerluck Jones* was somewhat different, for it did not actually imitate the Gillette play, but merely made fun of it, and people and organizations full of

ABOVE:
Sherlocko and Watso in The Robbery at the Railroad Station, *1912.*

RIGHT:
The original title was Who Done It?

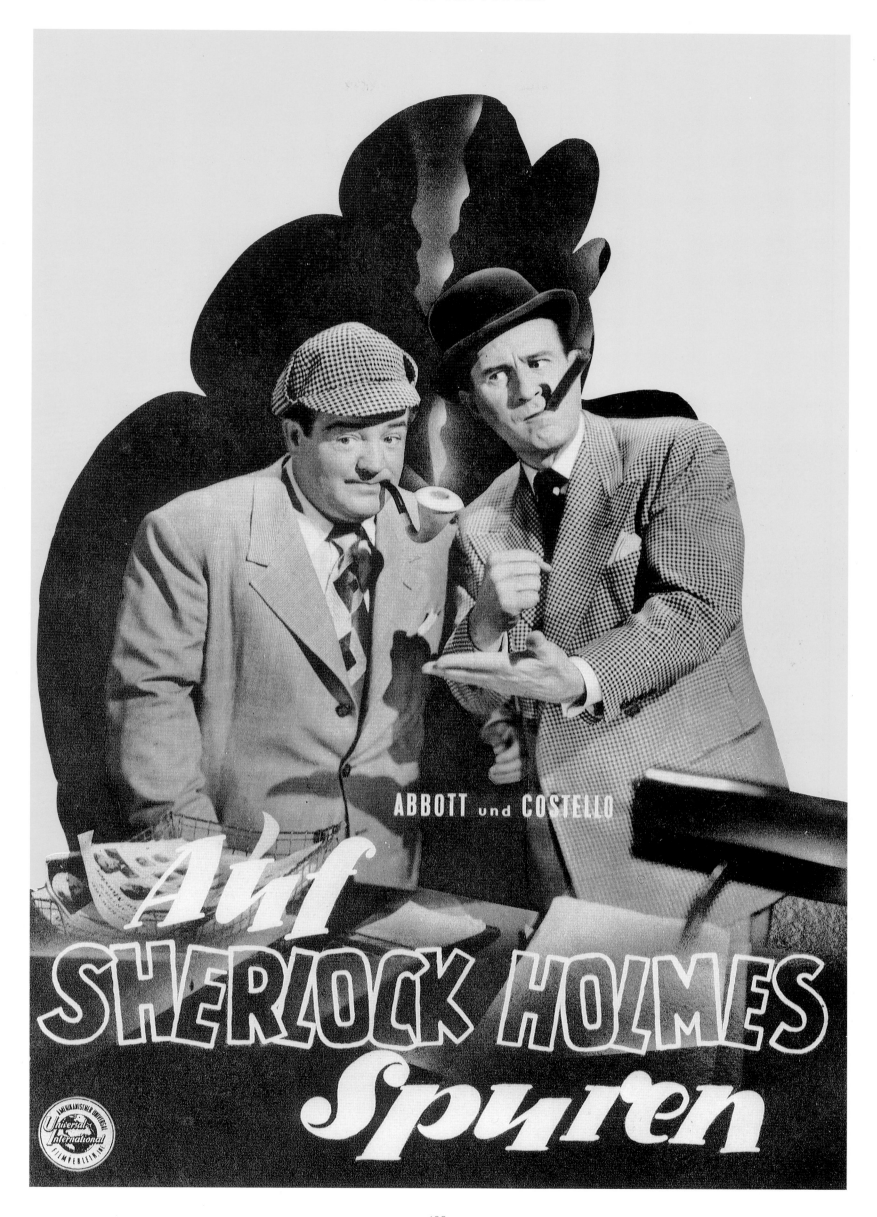

1902

THE SERVANT WATCHING THE SCARABEES   SHEERLUCK (MR. CLARENCE BLAKISTON) IN HIS CHAMBERS

"SHEERLUCK JONES," THE BURLESQUE OF "SHERLOCK HOLMES," AT TERRY'S THEATRE

"SHERLOCKO & WATSO"

The World Famous Sleuths in Champ Exclusive Pictures!

The first release on February 26th

"THE ROBBERY AT THE RAILROAD STATION"

introduces these strange but popular characters at their ingenious trade, solving a mystery surrounding the theft of a railroad lantern— A dark deed! See the film and learn how they solve it.

Do you realize what it will mean for you to advertise "SHER-LOCKO AND WATSO" for your theatre? Don't you see the profitable results? Of course you do, and you're not going to miss them!

Champion films are surpassed by none. The quality is there all the time. Every release in February with a Champ trade mark to it is a big feature.

"WRONGLY ACCUSED"

Released February 28th

ABOVE:
Sheerluck Jones, *an early stage spoof from the turn of the century.*

LEFT:
The grotesque make-up for Sherlocko and Watso was based on their appearance as drawn in comics. They even guyed the fancy dressing-gown!

RIGHT:
Best known among the early spoofs were the films featuring Mack Sennett and Fred Mace.

their own importance do not like that. *Sheerluck Jones* was written by the dramatic critics of the *Daily Telegraph*, Malcolm Watson, and the *Westminster Gazette*, Edward F. Spence, both of whom had criticized the production quite severely. '*Sheerluck Jones* caused a great deal of trouble,' wrote Spence in his autobiography, 'because the Lyceum management and Mr Gillette were very indignant about our "criticism in four paragraphs", for that was the descriptive term used by us. They seemed to think that it was bad form to make fun of them.'

Aside from some other minor flings at the now celebrated sleuth, the next humorous piece was, amazingly, by William Gillette himself. The stern and serious aspect of his portrayal of Sherlock Holmes had been emphasized by many critics, and by 1905 he probably felt securely enough established in his greatest role to be able to relax and have a little fun himself. He wrote and appeared in a little one-act episode that had several similar titles, but ended up as *The Painful Predicament of Sherlock Holmes*. In those days it was a frequent practice to present a short piece as a 'curtain-raiser' to the main play. *The Painful Predicament* was thus used, first in the USA and then in London, when Gillette returned with a play called *Clarice*, and sent to the provinces for the young Charles Chaplin, then touring in *Sherlock Holmes*, to play Billy at the Duke of York's Theater in St Martin's Lane. Apart from Billy, and Sherlock Holmes, the only other character in *The Painful Predicament* is Miss Gwendolyn Cobb, a lady who calls on Holmes and talks so much that he is unable to utter a word. In the process she drops his tobacco jar, treads on his violin, sits on the bow, smashes a chemistry retort and knocks over a lamp, all the while chattering incessantly. Holmes is finally rescued when two warders arrive to take her back to the asylum. Gillette's quiet irony was directed at critics of his vocal mannerisms by not speaking at all throughout the playlet.

On the cinema screen early film parodies were not impeded by any copyright restrictions, and comic versions of Sherlock Holmes abounded, almost invariably using the character in the customary slapstick comedies of the day, and appropriating the famous name, or a corruption of the name, as a box-office draw. Thus in quick succession there appeared *Sherlock Holmes Junior*, *A Squeedunk Sherlock Holmes*, *Hemlock Hoax*, *Charlie Colms*, *Baby Sherlock*, *Surelock Jones*, *Cousins of Sherlock Holmes*, *Homlock Shermes*, and so on, in their scores. Mack Sennett, of Keystone Kops fame, was responsible for a series of eleven films in two years, featuring himself and Fred Mace as 'The Sleuths', a pair of knockabout comic detectives in Sherlock Holmes garb.

As the cinema became a little more sophisticated, and as copyright laws were extended and enforced, the attempts at sending up the Holmes tradition on the screen became

scarcer, and more subtle, with selected incidents in both drama and comedy films in which characters briefly don the appropriate costume or emulate the conventional characteristics of Sherlock Holmes, or both. In sound films this has sometimes been achieved simply with some appropriate dialogue.

At Universal Studios, where the astonishing *Hellzapoppin'* had appeared in 1942, years ahead of its time as a wild, unprecedented style of comedy picture, it was easy to incorporate in the sequel *Crazy House* a scene in the Baker Street consulting room (a semi-permanent set on the Universal lot in those years) where Watson (Nigel Bruce) rushes in to tell

BIOGRAPH FILMS

Trade Mark Trade Mark

RELEASED OCTOBER 9th, 1911

ITALIAN BLOOD

An Illustration of What Might Have Been the Result of Indifference

In the little Italian home the wife feels she is neglected and apparently it seems that her husband's love is growing cold, for he has become decidedly indifferent. She, therefore, plans with her cousin to arouse his love through jealousy. At an Italian picnic, after repeated vain efforts to draw her husband's attentions toward her, she starts off with her cousin, passing in view of her husband. His fiery nature is violently aroused with jealousy, and rushing home in a towering rage would have wreaked disaster to the entire family, for his terrible suspicion poisons his mind even against his two little children. He learns the truth, however, and realizes now to what extreme the result of his neglect would have driven him.

Approximate Length 999 feet.

RELEASED OCTOBER 12th, 1911

Trailing the Counterfeiter

This is another big mystery, on which the two famous Biograph Sherlocks go to work. These two sleuths, as before, nearly catch the criminal. When they read in the newspapers of the mystery, they set out to solve it. They, of course, trail the wrong man, while real detectives run down the right one, and also arrest the sleuths for butting in. The police captain, however, lets them go, but later, when they, thinking they have discovered the crook's hiding place, blow in the wall of the police station, they are cooped up.

Approximate Length 529 feet.

JOSH'S SUICIDE

Josh doesn't like the way things go at home and decides to quit and get out. Later, his wife gets what purports to be his farewell letter, which is intended to lead her to believe he has committed suicide. He, however, goes to New York to have a good time, and he does "by gosh." The wife, believing herself a widow, makes a trip to New York with her admirer. Well, you may guess the rest. During the course of this little comedy many attractive New York scenes are shown.

Approximate Length 469 feet.

RELEASES FOR NEXT WEEK

October 16th, 1911
THE UNVEILING
Saving a Young Man from Moral, Social and Maybe Financial Ruin.
DRAMATIC
Approximate Length 998 feet.

October 19th, 1911
THE ADVENTURES OF BILLY
Suggested by Press Comment on the Tramp Evil.
DRAMATIC
Approximate Length 999 feet.

BIOGRAPH COMPANY, MOTION
11 East 14th Street, New York City

Licensees of the PICTURE PATENTS CO.
GEORGE KLEINE, Selling Agent for Chicago, 166 State Street, Chicago, Ill.

RIGHT & BELOW
Neither Lou Costello (right) nor Harpo Marx (below) seem to be aware that in America the deerstalker is often called a fore-and-aft cap, since they are each wearing one port-and-starboard.

ABOVE:
*Justin Playfair (George C Scott)
imagines he is Sherlock Holmes. Dr
Mildred Watson (Joanne
Woodward)* knows *she is Dr
Watson.* They Might Be Giants,
1971.

Holmes (Rathbone) that the dreaded Olsen and Johnson are coming, to which the omniscient Holmes responds that he knows, because he is Sherlock Holmes and knows everything. This type of in-joke is uncommon, and most treatments within films have been as described in the previous paragraph.

The first time a feature film was completely devoted to a humorous form of the Sherlock Holmes syndrome was *They Might Be Giants* (1971). Originally a partially successful play by James Goldman, it was filmed by Universal (where there must be a soft spot for Holmes) with George C Scott as Justin Playfair, a wealthy lawyer who is suffering from a nervous breakdown and goes about in cape and deerstalker, believing he is Sherlock Holmes. His family, hoping to get him certified so they can get their hands on his fortune, send him to a psychiatrist named Dr Mildred Watson, played by Joanne Woodward, but meeting Dr Watson simply convinces him that he *is* Holmes. It was a highly amusing, original and entertaining treatment of Holmes and Watson, spoiled only by being heavily edited just before release, which made the ending incomprehensible.

In an extraordinary choice, the BBC presented in 1973 what was described as 'the first ever licensed send-up of Sherlock Holmes' with their Comedy Playhouse production of *Elementary My Dear Watson*, which was afflicted with the manic John Cleese (of Monty Python fame) as Holmes. Apparently it was intended as a pilot program for a series that never materialized. The only mystery was why it was authorized by the

LEFT:
Holmes and Watson find a client.

FAR RIGHT:
Playfair's family assert that he is 'up the pole,' but Mildred Watson is not so sure.

RIGHT:
Piet Bambergen starred with a basset hound in the rather bizarre Dutch comedy, De dwaze lotgevallon van Sherlock Jones *(The Crazy Adventures of Sherlock Holmes) in 1975.*

De dwaze lotgevallen van

SHERLOCK JONES

TOP LEFT:
After a lapse of ten years, Douglas Wilmer reappeared as Holmes in The Adventures of Sherlock Holmes' Smarter Brother. *Here Thorley Walters as Dr Watson helps Holmes get his brother out of trouble.*

RIGHT:
Sigi Holmes, the alleged smarter sibling, was played by Gene Wilder, who also wrote and directed the movie.

BOTTOM LEFT:
Sigi Holmes was assisted by the goggle-eyed Sergeant Orville Sacker from Scotland Yard, played by Marty Feldman.

Conan Doyle Estate at all.

Equally unappealing was *The Adventure of Sherlock Holmes's Smarter Brother*, a forcible demonstration of just how not to make fun of the Sherlock Holmes phenomenon. There was a moment in the film when a disastrous performance of Verdi's opera *A Masked Ball* is taking place, and the camera is positioned with the audience in the stalls, looking over the backs of heads. One of the heads turns round and addresses the camera. It is an uncredited Albert Finney, who asks 'Is this rotten, or wonderfully brave?' He might well have been referring to the film as a whole, which was both rotten and wonderfully foolhardy. Presumably intended to follow on the lines of film director Mel Brooks's send-ups of Broadway (*The Producers*), The Western (*Blazing Saddles*) and the horror movie (*Young Frankenstein*), in all of which Gene Wilder appeared, the film of *Smarter Brother* had the Mel Brooks team without Brooks, and there seemed to be very little close consideration of the problems of burlesquing Sherlock Holmes, and no realization that sending up a genre is nothing like so daunting a task as tackling an institution.

Smarter Brother did not even come to grips with the subject, and made little attempt to live up to its title, for Sigi Holmes, the younger brother, is not only *not* smarter (and the word 'smarter' was emphasized in the title in all the publicity), but has to be helped by Sherlock more than once. The idea of an insanely jealous younger brother wishing to put one over on Sherlock has good humorous possibilities that were not realized in this film, which lacked the development and polish we might expect from more experienced directors. Younger brother Sigi was played by the writer and director of the film, Gene Wilder, who made virtually no concession to the period, the conventions or the Englishness of the subject in his performance, which was given in his customary demented and unrelated style. Douglas Wilmer, a former Sherlock Holmes on BBC television in 1965, had the same role in *Smarter Brother*, but really had little to do but just look the part, as did Thorley Walters as Dr Watson. At least for those two competent actors their time on the screen was relatively brief.

So far as is known, Holland has never produced a Sherlock Holmes film, and as the Granada series is being shown there it seems unlikely to happen, but in 1975 a comedy film called *The Crazy Adventures of Sherlock Jones* was made, with Dutchman Piet Bambergen in the title role. Film expert Geoff Donaldson of Rotterdam wrote: 'The hero of this film is a would-be detective who becomes involved with the Mafia and a stolen diamond. Thanks to his trusty (and far more intelligent) assistant, a bassett hound called Watson, he manages to solve the case. The film was a flop, mainly because of a

ABOVE:
Douglas Wilmer.

TOP RIGHT:
The 'world's greatest detectives'
without the founder member.

BOTTOM RIGHT:
Sherman Holmes (Larry Hagman)
in The Return of the World's
Greatest Detective.

weak script and the fact that the director couldn't control the antics of the comedian Piet Bambergen, but the dog gave a lovely performance!'

Neil Simon's *Murder by Death* (1976) presents a mystery all of its own, for some copies of the film are alleged to have the characters of Holmes and Watson while most copies do not. The story as written by Simon is a satire on famous fictional detectives, and includes take-offs of Hercule Poirot, Sam Spade, Miss Marple, Charlie Chan and Nick and Nora Charles, so it seems incredible that Holmes and Watson should not be included. As originally written and filmed, the story is supposed to have shown Holmes and Watson arriving late at a mansion party at which all the other sleuths have attended, and have failed to solve the inevitable murder. Holmes then solves the crime but departs without divulging the answer to the others. The actors impersonating the other detectives objected so strongly to being upstaged by Holmes, both as a latecomer in the film and as played by a lesser-known performer, that a different ending was written and filmed, and Holmes and Watson deleted. Apparently some copies with the original ending have been shown in some states in the USA.

While all this was going on, or not going on, in the cinema in 1976, television in America had two further oblique approaches to Holmes. ABC Television produced a weekly series *Holmes and Yoyo*, in which Richard Schull played a regular police detective named Holmes, who had as his partner a six-million-dollar-type humanoid robot, played by John Schuck. The twist was that Holmes was a conventional cop, with Yoyo frequently providing the clever deductions; a good amusing series, even if only aimed at juvenile audiences. NBC Television's contribution was *The Return of the World's*

Greatest Detective, in which Larry Hagman (better known as the World's Greatest Heel – J R Ewing) plays a dumb motorcycle cop, Sherman Holmes, whose bike falls on him while he is reclining in a park reading Sherlock Holmes stories. When he comes to he is convinced he *is* Sherlock Holmes, and is helped by a pretty psychiatric social worker whose name is Watson. Sounds familiar? That's because it's the plot of *They Might Be Giants* all over again, and, plagiarism aside, none the worse for retelling.

As if the unappealing *Elementary My Dear Watson* had not warned him off, John Cleese was back as Holmes again in 1977 in *The Strange Case of the End of Civilization As We Know It*. To be more precise he was Arthur Sherlock Holmes, grandson of Sherlock, teamed up with Arthur Lowe as the grandson of Watson, in an ambitious mixture of political satire and a brief fantasia of fictional detectives (namely Hercule Poirot, Columbo, Steve McGarrett, Sam Spade and McCloud). If *that* sounds familiar, it was not in fact a re-hash of *Murder By Death*, but rather a script that had a number of bright moments not helped by variable direction. Some of the jokes were variable too (Watson, doing a crossword puzzle: 'Simple source of citrus fruit?' Holmes: 'A lemon tree, my dear Watson'), and the script was plainly fashioned to provide a total buffoon in Watson, to serve as the object of John Cleese's familiar performance of extreme exasperation.

When one is debunking something, the piling on of absurdities is perfectly justified if the result is at all funny. In the case of *The Hound of the Baskervilles*, as directed by Paul Morrissey, the result was an undisciplined mess of ancient jokes, lavatory humor and amateurish self-indulgent horseplay, perpetrated by Peter Cook (Holmes) and Dudley Moore (Watson) with no visible signs of shame. Paul Morrissey, who

ABOVE:
Terry-Thomas, Kenneth Williams, Dudley Moore and Peter Cook as Dr Mortimer, Sir Henry Baskerville, Watson, and Holmes.

RIGHT:
Holmes, Watson and The Hound of the Baskervilles, *1979*

TOP LEFT:
John Cleese, weighed down by anxiety and a calabash.

LEFT:
The grandsons of Holmes and Watson (John Cleese and Arthur Lowe in The Strange Case of the End of Civilization As We Know It, *1977.*

LEFT:
Michael Caine and Ben Kingsley,
Without a Clue, *1989.*

TOP RIGHT:
*Ben Kingsley, Michael Caine and a
twisted calabash.*

BOTTOM RIGHT:
*Not a lot of people know that
Sherlock Holmes was really a
drunken actor named Kincaid.*

once made films for Andy Warhol, professed great admiration for the British *Carry On* films, clearly unaware that the old Carry On team could have made a far better humorous *Hound*, and probably cheaper, too. After this, denounced by one writer as the worst Holmes film ever made, the Conan Doyle Estate may have decided that enough was enough, for no further licensed send-ups were made.

Even after 1980, when the Doyle copyrights expired in Britain and Europe, no further satires of note were produced, until in 1989 when *Without a Clue* attempted to give a fresh twist to the Holmesian theme. Dr Watson, the brilliant deductive reasoner and author of the accounts appearing in *The Strand Magazine*, is required to produce the amazing hero of his stories, and hires a dissipated out-of-work actor named Reginald Kincaid to act as Sherlock Holmes. They become involved in investigating a major crime which proves to be the handiwork of Professor Moriarty, and the climax includes a swordfight between the Professor and Kincaid/Holmes. (A duel with swords appears to be a stock device to fall back on in recent films, with fencing galore in *The Adventure of Sherlock Holmes' Smarter Brother*, also in *The Seven-Per-Cent Solution*).

Clearly the achievement of *They Might Be Giants*, and for that matter Billy Wilder's *The Private Life of Sherlock Holmes*, was due to the respect and even affection shown towards the original subject, and like all good dramas the better serious Sherlock Holmes plays and films have been enhanced by the occasional and judicious introduction of humor, and even whimsy. What most of the other attempts at parody have failed to recognize is that a really successful outcome will not be attained by knockabout farce and tasteless vulgarity.

Michael Caine usually has a ready answer for interviewers. When *Without a Clue* was first announced, it was put to him that with his Cockney accent he was an unlikely choice for Holmes. 'Ah,' replied Caine, 'that's why they're calling it *The Imposter of Baker Street.*'

CHAPTER 6
THE GREAT AMUSERS
AND
PERSUADERS

LIKE THE SERIOUS imperso- nators, it did not take long for comedians and comic-strip artists to latch on to Sherlock Holmes as a potential source of fun. As already indicated in Chapter 5, *The Adventures of Chubb-Lock Homes* first appeared in a humorous British weekly periodical known as *Comic Cuts*, in November 1893. *Comic Cuts*, selling at one halfpenny, helped to fill a want of the man in the street for cheap, light, easy-to-read literature that was not constantly preaching at him. Readers were evidently able to appreciate the skit on Sherlock Holmes, since Chubb-Lock continued to appear until September 1894, being found in 33 issues in all. At first Chubb-Lock did not appear every week, and on his second appearance somebody blundered, and the strip was printed with the heading *Sherlock Holmes*, but that appears to have happened only once.

In 1911 'Sherlocko and Watso' were established in America as comic strip characters, somewhat on the lines of the famous Mutt and Jeff, and in 1912 they made the transition from comic strip to movies in at least two comedy films, in which the Champion Film Company produced close likenesses of their grotesque appearance. Also in America, in 1929, the celebrated Joe Archibald produced the first of a series of strips featuring *Shylock Bones* in the first issue of *The Funnies*.

More frequent are the individual cartoons with one-line joke captions, and many of these have been ingenious in their graphic wit, while others have merely become dated, as the examples demonstrate. Similarly on the cinema screen there have been various cartoon films with the customary take-offs, an early one being the ever-fascinating Felix the Cat in *Surelock Homes* in the 1920s, while in 1928 Walt Disney joined in the fun with *Mickey the Detective*. In conventional films there were numerous short jokes, visual or verbal or both, in various dramas and comedy films. Some were a little

subtle in their allusions to Holmes and Watson, while many were bordering on the slapstick, as can be seen from some of the illustrations.

A marginal but pleasantly charming cartoon film made by the Walt Disney Studios in 1986 was *Basil, the Great Mouse Detective*, based on the children's books by Eve Titus about Basil, the mouse who dwells beneath the floorboards in Baker Street and who, in this film, becomes involved with a rodent Moriarty named Professor Ratigan (voice deliciously supplied by Vincent Price).

SHYLOCK BONES

By Joe Archibald

Sherlocko and Watso

Already Favorites

in the public eye, will appear in Champion pictures, in special dashing, laugh-convulsive Comedies. We have the exclusive privilege for this feature. Therefore, every exhibitor must employ every means for booking this

Cash Box Delight.

The Champion Film Co.

MARK M. DINTENFASS, Gen'l Mgr.

Now located in new offices at

145 West 45th St.   New York City

The Week's Releases

For Monday, Dec. 25th, 1911

"Bonnie Of The Hills"

Parted from her sweetheart, Bonnie leaves her western home to educate herself at an Academy. A subsequent meeting and auto ride leads to their hold-up by bandits. Bonnie cleverly outwits and captures them. The sweethearts are then re-united.

For Wednesday, December 27th, 1911

"The Doctor's Close Call"

A young doctor, seeking to recover his health in the West, is captured in the company of bandits. His faithful sweetheart back East reads of his peril and courageously saves him.

Robert G. Fowler

The Renowned Aviator

accompanied by a Champion camera man, is making an interesting air cruise from New Orleans to the Atlantic seaboard. Fascinating scenic pictures of beautiful and pleasing value. Overhead city flights will also be included.

Digest This News?

TOP:
A popular comic strip from the 1920s, Shylock Bones.

ABOVE:
Sherlocko and Watso as they appeared in this comic form.

RIGHT:
Basil, the Great Mouse Detective, 1986.

LEFT:
An undated, unauthorized French adventure involving Holmes with Raffles, who was the creation of Doyle's brother-in-law, E W Hornung.

A "Sweep" in playing The New Game "Sherlock Holmes".

PURE, LAUGHABLE, EXCITING FUN

The GAME
Sherlock Holmes

LAUGHABLE EXCITING
Entirely **NEW**
For Any Number
EASILY LEARNED

RULES FOR PLAYING THE GAME OF

Sherlock Holmes
(Registered Trademark)

Copyright, 1904, by
PARKER BROTHERS, Inc.
SALEM, MASS., U. S. A.
*Sole Makers of Sherlock Holmes, Pit, Pillow-Dex,
Ping-Pong, etc.*
FLATIRON BUILDING, NEW YORK
11 LOVELL'S CT., PATERNOSTER ROW, LONDON, E. C., ENG.

IDEA of the GAME

The play of the game is simple and very exciting, and is entirely new. Any number, from three to eight, can take part. The object is to capture as many "Burglars," "Robbers," and "Thieves" cards as possible. *All players play at once* and there is not a dull moment. A large part of the fun of the game consists in turning up the card "Sherlock Holmes," and seizing the playing piles of opponents.

RULES
COPYRIGHT 1904 BY PARKER BROTHERS

(1) Shuffle the cards and deal the entire pack.

(2) Take the cards dealt to you in one hand, *without looking at them, keeping them faces towards the palm.*

(3) The Dealer begins the game by calling "READY – PLAY." When he calls **"PLAY"** each player, the dealer included, must take the upper card from his hand, and quickly play it, face up, upon the table in front of him, without glancing at face of the card until it is on the table.

BELOW & LEFT:
Family games featuring Sherlock Holmes have not been confined to English-speaking countries. Since the Doyle copyright expired in Britain there has been a steady introduction of new board games like these.

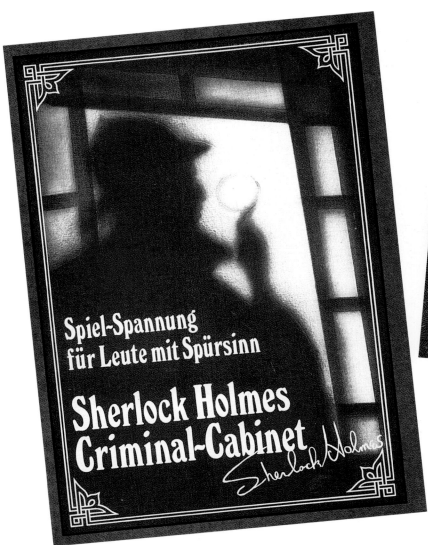

ABOVE:
The Sherlock Holmes stories have rightly been elevated to 'classics', in both the worlds of hardback and comic books.

TOP RIGHT:
Sherlock Holmes even became involved in an improbable encounter with Batman's famous adversary The Joker in 1976, while on the far right a 1952 Mexican translation of a Conan Doyle story uses Bruce and Rathbone on the cover.

BOTTOM RIGHT:
The Hound of the Baskervilles, *as interpreted by Classics Illustrated in English and in Greek, 1947.*

LILLIPUT

"I think a little unobtrusive mingling with the crowd at the jewellery counter is indicated, Grimshaw . . ."

321

Punch, April 16 1947

"Dick Barton! Tchah!"

ABOVE:
The reference to Dick Barton's daily radio adventures was not lost on British listeners in 1947.

SHERLOCK HOLMES . . . *The new daily adventure strip starts today*

EVENING STANDARD   MONDAY, MARCH 1, 1954

SHERLOCK HOLMES

THURSDAY, MARCH 4, 1954

On television, of course, Sherlock Holmes has proved invaluable as material for comedy sketches in the innumerable shows starring so-called funny men. A few of them really are funny but many are only as successful as the work of their team of script-writers enables them to be, and it sometimes seems that there is a slogan on the writer's wall reading 'If all else fails, try a Sherlock Holmes skit.'

The same phrase seems to appeal to copywriters, too. Frequent use has been made of the name, the character or just the trade marks (deerstalker, pipe etc) in advertisements in

magazines and newspapers, as well as on television and in the cinema (mostly, one suspects, without authorization).

Linking a well-known name to the selling of a product must have started around the same time that advertising began. Recommendations from satisfied customers are always valuable, especially when the customer is famous or distinguished, but a fictional character cannot endorse a commodity or provide an unsolicited testimonial as to its worth. So the use of such a character requires careful consideration, and is probably best achieved with the benefit of humor. Some

As one of fiction's greatest smokers,
it is not surprising that
Sherlock Holmes has been used
to promote tobacco.

Sherlock Holmes :

"No help here, Watson. No smears, no scratching, no sign of finger prints. They evidently use RONUK in this household."

(With apologies to Sir A. Conan Doyle.)

RONUK FURNITURE CREAM

Easiest — Goes furthest — Lasts longest.
Blue Stone Jars 10d., 1/7½.   Glass Bottles 9d., 1/6.
RONUK, LTD., PORTSLADE, SUSSEX.

LEFT:
Not only an acknowledgment to Conan Doyle, but an illustration not unworthy of the stories, June 1926.

BELOW:
Copyright had only just expired when Listerine joined the horde of advertisers adopting the idea.

TOP RIGHT:
The characters seem confused in this dialogue, but see page 141.

BOTTOM RIGHT:
This most important advertisement appeared in the program of William Gillette's play at the Lyceum in 1901.

NICE LOGIC, SHAME ABOUT THE BREATH.

It was after the appointed hour. 6.33 p.m.
Unlike Holmes to be late. Watson whistled to keep up his courage.
A gaunt shadow snarled and flickered its way across the hall. A thick, stale odour permeated the landing.
At that very moment, Watson knew.
His revered and trusted companion had forgotten his daily gargle with Listerine Mouthwash.
(Brushing your teeth just isn't enough to kill the germs that can cause bad breath.)
Thinking about it afterwards, Watson found it odd that so logical a man could have overlooked something so elementary.

Listerine Antiseptic Mouthwash.
It's enough to take your breath away.

Clueless 'tec becomes a Baker Street 'regular'

NEVER met a man with less clues than Hobson. "Found any new bodies lately?" I asked him.

"I'd swap mine for any I did find," said Hobson. "Anything to be rid of this constipation. As a detective, I make a pretty good pipe-rack—and that's all!"

"Pipe wreck, I'd say." I said.

"Huh?" growled Hobson.

"S'right," I said. "I visualize a case of chaos in that 30 feet of piping you have inside you. Everything you eat has to pass along it, and your intestinal muscles are there to jolly it along. But they've nothing to pull on in the sort of food we eat nowadays—too soft and starchy."

"Then what happens?" rasped Hobson.

"A sudden arrest," I said, "with no further developments expected. In fact, you're constipated—and the reason is lack of bulk in your diet,"

"What is bulk?" asked Hobson.

"Kellogg's All-Bran!" I said triumphantly. "It's bulk, it's a delightful breakfast-food, and it's what you need. All-Bran'll make you regular in a few days."

"You'd better be right," hissed Hobson.

Exit a tired 'tec, and re-enter, three days later, a super-sleuth—a Big 5 Hobson.

"Warroo!" he yodelled. "I feel a new man. That All-Bran really has made me 'regular.' What's the secret of this wonderful food?"

"Alimentary, my dear Hobson," I said.

*   *   *

KELLOGG'S ALL-BRAN relieves constipation, keeps you "regular." Made from rich outer layers of whole wheat, deliciously oven-toasted with salt, malt, and sugar. Makes a splendid breakfast, and many appetizing cakes, buns, and surprise dishes.

8½d. a packet, from your grocer.

---

of the best advertisements incorporating Sherlock Holmes have utilized a gentle, tongue-in-cheek approach which seems more fitting, but who can really tell how effective such a choice of advertisement has been? Market researchers will nowadays produce all sorts of convincing statistics and tables to prove or disprove the value of a particular advertising campaign, but it seems very likely that many of us are less easily led than the persuaders would have us believe. We often remember a clever advertisement, but for the life of us cannot recall what the product was. That factor does not seem to have discouraged advertisers from adopting Sherlock Holmes from very early days in the appearance of the stories.

One of the earliest advertisements (and no doubt other contenders of an earlier date will be found) appeared in the *Illustrated London News* of 20 January 1894, the month after the story *The Final Problem* had appeared in *The Strand Magazine*, and readers were mourning the presumed death of their hero. It was opportunism of the highest degree, and a smart piece of copy-writing by Beechams Pills, noted for their wordy treatments of a tricky subject in countless magazine and newspaper advertisements over many years.

The overt deployment of Sherlock Holmes, with or without Dr Watson, has continued ever since, and there can be few products or services that have not been a party to the use, or misuse of those characters. Sadly many of the advertisements have been devised in such a heavy-handed manner that it is clear that a number of unsubtle advertising agencies and artists have had little or no idea how to make good use of a character who is instantly recognizable. Since 1894 there can have been few products or services that have not been advertised with pictures of, or references to Sherlock Holmes, from insurance to motor tires. Some companies have produced a

The Re-appearance of Sherlock Holmes

SHERLOCK HOLMES, the eminent "specialist in crime," will be hailed with delight by the many thousands of readers who, ten years ago were enthralled by Dr. CONAN DOYLE'S masterly telling of the expert detective's wonderful achievements. The weird mysteries he solved, the strange histories he unravelled, and the plans he followed in deciphering unheard-of problems, scientific and criminal, fascinated multitudes the whole world over then, as never before or since, through the pages of the 'Strand' Magazine.

Readers of to-day may also revel in the unexpected developments that follow in rapid succession as the "man with eyes at the back of his head" discovers clue after clue of the mystery which enshrouds the gruesome legend of . . .

"The Hound of the Baskervilles."

The ingenious deductions of Sherlock Holmes; the thrilling passages of this weirdly interesting history carry one forward with exhilarating force in the effort to keep pace with the constantly changing scenes of the great detective's latest adventure. The opening chapters were given in the August number and the story is continued to a critical point . . .

In the Sept. 'STRAND' Magazine 6d. Now Selling.

Sherlock Holmes:—
"Judging by the line of evidence,
there's a Lady in that house!"

ABOVE & RIGHT:
*Judging by current market values,
picture postcards and cigarette
cards have a vastly enhanced
attraction whenever Sherlock
Holmes is depicted.*

432 **WILLIAM GILLETTE.**
Impersonating "Sherlock Holmes."

Ogden's *Guinea Gold* Cigarettes.

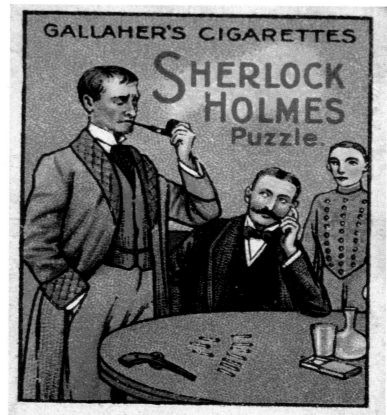

GALLAHER'S CIGARETTES

SHERLOCK HOLMES Puzzle.

Arrange 10 matches in such a manner to form 5 rows with four matches in each row.

Nº 64

PLAYER'S CIGARETTES.

SHERLOCK HOLMES.
"THE ADVENTURES OF SHERLOCK HOLMES."

CONAN DOYLE CHARACTERS
SHERLOCK HOLMES

CONAN DOYLE CHARACTERS
DR. WATSON

CONAN DOYLE CHARACTERS
SHERLOCK HOLMES DISGUISED

CONAN DOYLE CHARACTERS
LESTRADE

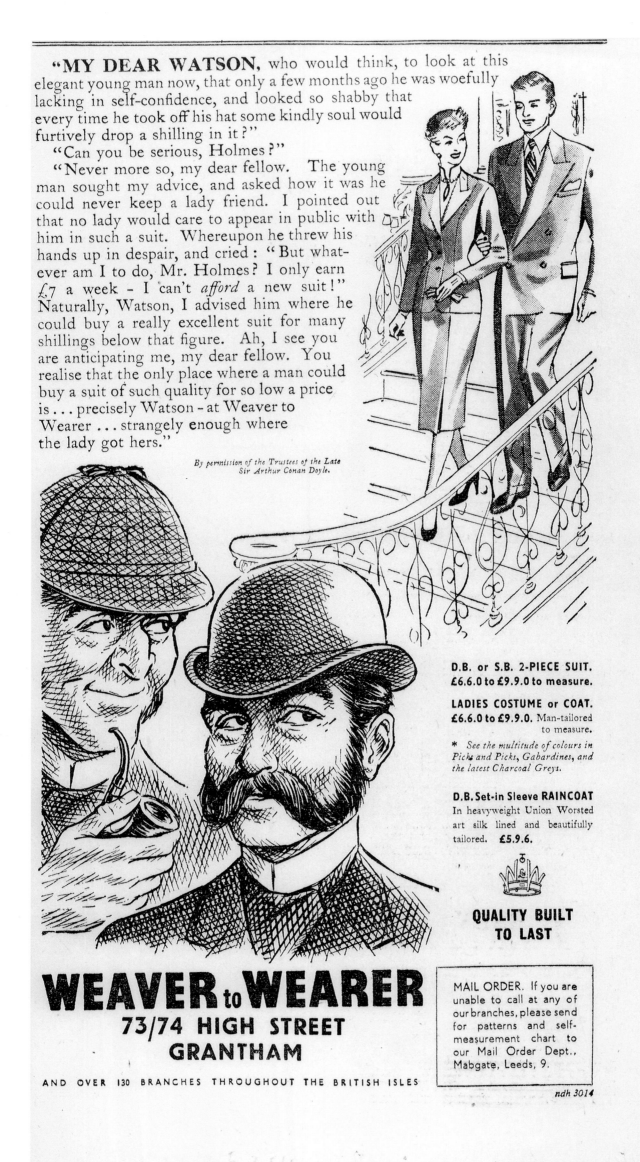

RIGHT:
In 1949 The Strand Magazine itself invoked the assistance of Sherlock Holmes in promoting sales, but to no avail: the magazine expired two years later.

BELOW & LEFT:
Few commodities seem to have missed the chance to use the celebrated characters to sell to the public, including ready-made suits in Britain, and shirts in America.

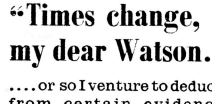

"Times change, my dear Watson...

....or so I venture to deduce from certain evidence brought to my notice. Not a hansom in Baker Street. Not a gaslight in Piccadilly. And as for the Strand—"

"*Your observation astounds me, Holmes. When last I visited the Strand—*"

"I was talking, my dear fellow, not of the estimable thoroughfare of that name, but of the equally famous 'Strand Magazine,' in whose pages you and I once cut such prominent figures. It is, as always, a most excellent magazine. But modernised, Watson, modernised. A new 'Strand', rich in the pith and movement of the times, full of good writing and illustration. In the January number, for example, John Dickson Carr, tells the real-life story of how our revered creator, Conan Doyle, himself solved a notorious criminal case—applying *my* methods."

"*You intrigue me, Holmes. I—*"

"But that is merely one item. There are many other good things—brilliant short stories, topical articles, delectable colour features. Yes, the 'Strand' may have changed with the times, Watson, but its old quality goes on for ever. I strongly advocate that you purchase a copy this very day."

Look Watson—the shirt for Britain with a dash of American

LEFT:
Jeremy Young in The Case of the Fantastical Pass Book, *Abbey National Building Society, 1979.*

ABOVE:
Jeremy Clyde (Holmes), Ken Halliwell (Watson), and Hugh Laurie in the Video Arts training film When Can You Start?, *1988.*

RIGHT:
Once copyright had expired, Kelloggs were able to use the name of Sherlock Holmes without restraint.
See page 135.

short series of advertisements with little cases unfailingly solved by Holmes, with the product in the punchline, to the perpetual astonishment of Watson. In this type of advertisement it usually turns out that the illustrations are a lot better than the text. Many of the advertisements simply rely on the 'Amazing – Elementary' exchange between the two characters to frame an otherwise unconnected straight sell.

In more recent times, following the introduction of color magazines and color television, there have been some very elaborate set-ups purporting to be Victorian backgrounds, against which Holmes and Watson unravel a little mystery and boost the product. Again, the costumes and color photography are frequently the most interesting aspect. Now that the Sherlock Holmes stories are in the public domain, so far as Britain and Europe are concerned, there seems little doubt that we shall see a great deal more of Holmes and Watson; the products and services with which their names will be associated will continue to amuse, amaze or anger us.

SHERLOCK HOLMES AND THE MYSTERY OF THE VANISHING *CRUNCHY NUT CORN FLAKES.*

—?—

"Good grief Holmes! It's happened again. This box of Crunchy Nut Corn Flakes was full only yesterday—it's half empty already!"

"I suspect someone has been eating them, Watson."

"Good heavens, Holmes, do you really think so? How do you propose to uncover the culprit?"

"Elementary my dear Watson—those golden flakes of corn encrusted with brown sugar, nuts & honey are quite irresistible. The miscreant will be wearing a very contented expression."

"I see you have the case well under control, Holmes, no wonder you're looking so pleased. But who would do such a dastardly thing as to take a man's breakfast? This is serious Holmes. We must look for clues... Holmes...?"

"Yes my dear Watson?"

"..There's a flake of cereal on your lapel...Good heavens Holmes, you don't think the villain's trying to frame you...?"

For answers to any questions you have concerning health, or for information on local and national health services or support groups, contact–

VICTORIA HEALTH CENTRE · GLASSHOUSE S^T

NOTTINGHAM · NGI 3LW · ☎ NOTT^M 480500

ABOVE:
*Not only Sherlock Holmes, but also
some of the Sidney Paget
illustrations have been appropriated
for advertising from time to time.*

RIGHT:
*Smoking has continued to be
associated with Holmes, but Singing
Cigarettes?*

PERFECT COPIES...THE FT4060

My dear Watson, don't get excited. You see how fiendishly clever these Ricoh people are: the merest touch on the controls and the machine runs. And here, observe, another clever touch, an INTEGRATED SORTER, as well as a Document Feeder. What's this you say Watson? Dry toner, A3 plain paper to A6 postcard, and reductions and enlargement as well? Quite so. Very impressive of course – what do you expect from the world's largest manufacturer of copiers?

Brief investigation reveals the following:–
Speed – 20 copies/minute; desk-top; original size up to A3; copy size A6 (105 x 148 mm) to A3 (297 x 420mm); exact 1:1 reproduction plus reduction and enlargement. Paper feed from dual cassettes with optional by-pass feed.

Mail the coupon. Dr Watson thinks you should do this as a matter of some urgency! Find out why 20,000 were installed in the first four months in Japan alone!
Ricoh UK Limited, Ricoh House, 32 Stephenson Way, London NW1. Tel: 01-388 3200

Name
Title
Company Address

Tel No
BED/15

RICOH
TECHNOLOGY WITH A HUMAN TOUCH

INSTANT INFO Circle No. 407

Good quality artwork and costly colour reproduction (left) do not make up for weak copy, whereas the advertisement on the right starts with a clever idea and follows it through. The Ward ad is 1986 and Ricoh 1983.

These advertisements from the 1950s exemplify the simplistic use of the ever-familiar image. It is doubtful that many of these at that time used Sherlock Holmes with permission.

Elementary— my dear Watson

I NEVER THOUGHT OF THAT is the first reaction of many people when we mention that *Lloyds Bank Travellers' Cheques* are just as useful *here at home* as they are abroad. Yet it does not take a Sherlock Holmes to perceive the similarity of the two cases. It is very convenient, anywhere, to pay one's way by Travellers' Cheques — hotel bills, rail tickets, air or boat passages. And even more so to be able to re-fill one's note-case judiciously from time to time instead of cramming it from the outset with highly-transferable wealth.

Lloyds Bank Travellers' Cheques can be cashed at the branches of most British Banks and are widely accepted throughout Britain by many other agents. The security and consequent ease of mind they provide are invaluable.

LLOYDS BANK TRAVELLERS' CHEQUES

Ask at any branch of the Bank for full details of these facilities

SHERLOCK HOLMES invariably knew Just where to look for a clue. How useful now his cool deductions In tracking down those Armour Star productions.

— means best in food!

ARMOUR & COMPANY LIMITED, LONDON, E.C.1

In a rare appearance in an industrial film made for the British Electricity Council in 1972, Sherlock Holmes 'enters the technological age and introduces his friend to the wide range of applications of metal sheathed heating elements'. Skilfully produced by the Larkins Studio, the film combined animated cartoons and live action industrial scenes.

SHERLOCK HOLMES SOCIETY OF AUSTRALIA
P.O. BOX 13, STIRLING, 5152

50th Anniversary Tawny Springton Port

"It is a good wine, Holmes"
"A remarkable wine, Watson"

Commemorating the 50th anniversary of the death of Sir Arthur Conan Doyle on the 7th July 1930

PRODUCED BY L. F. & L. K. HOLMES, MOUNT PLEASANT
750 ml
ALCOHOL 18.2% BY VOLUME
PRODUCE OF SOUTH AUSTRALIA

From advertisements, it was but a short step to using the Holmesian identity marks on the products themselves. Gin from Spain, tobacco from Denmark, mineral water from the well at what is now called 221B Baker Street, London, and port from South Australia are some of the goods marketed in this fashion.

ABOVE:
*In 1978 artist Ken Taylor produced
a clever comic strip that only
reveals itself as an advertisement in
the penultimate frame.*

BELOW:
*Other forms of entertainment have embraced
Sherlock Holmes besides showbiz. This is The Hound of
the Baskervilles diarama at Madame Tussaud's,
located, coincidentally, in Baker Street.*

With great imagination, London
Transport seized the opportunity of
the refurbishing of the Baker Street
Underground station to honor the
street's most famous resident. Scenes
from various stories are used to
decorate the platforms.

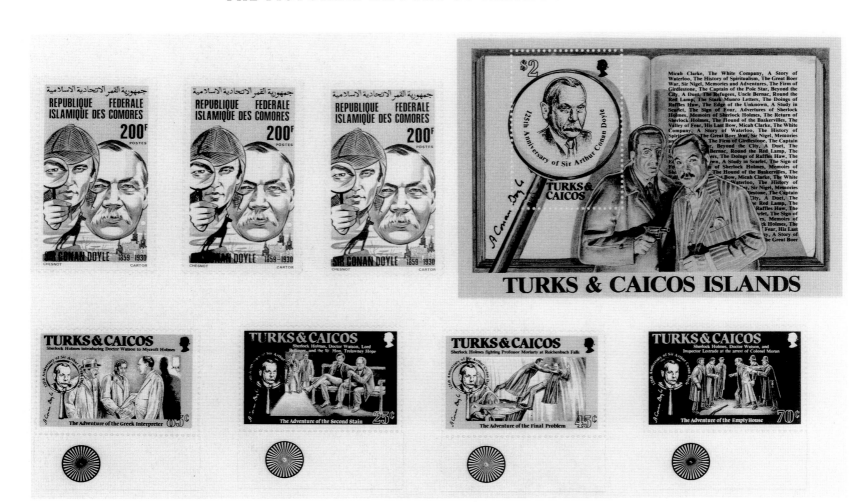

In 1984 the Turks & Caicos Islands issued the boldest series of
stamps featuring both Conan Doyle and Sherlock Holmes. The
tiny Republic of Comores, similarly issued one stamp on which for
once Doyle achieved slightly greater prominence than Holmes,
who years before had appeared on a stamp from Nicaragua. The
British Post Office, however, has so far only managed some
meagre stamp covers, printed at a quarter of the size shown here.

MY DEAR WATSON
THE COFFEE HOUSE OF DISTINCTION

PREVIOUS PAGE:
*Since the 1950s the Sherlock Holmes pub
has been a center of attraction in Northumberland
Avenue, and remains a fitting place
of pilgrimage for Holmesian visitors to London.*

LEFT:
*The Sherlock Holmes Hotel in
Baker Street is a good example of
the architecture of the street
applicable to the period of the stories.*

ABOVE:
*The 'My Dear Watson' coffee bar
lasted only a few years in Baker Street.*

RIGHT:
*Moriarty's, a bar situated within
the entrance of Baker Street
station, was forced to close when
London Transport prohibited the
sale of alcohol anywhere on their premises.
A judgment on the name, perhaps?*

BELOW:
Yet another commercial variant of the great name.

**The Secretary to Sherlock Holmes,
Abbey National Building Society,
221b Baker Street,
London.**

Dear Reader,

Letters addressed to Sherlock Holmes have been answered by the staff of the Abbey National Building Society for over fifty years and I am the latest to serve as his secretary.

The head office, Abbey House, stands in Baker Street and includes the number 221 which many would say is the site of the rooms which Holmes shared with Dr Watson. The present building was opened in 1932 as the headquarters of what was then the Abbey Road Building Society, but which in 1944 took its present name following the merger with the National Building Society. In 1951 it housed the Sherlock Holmes Exhibition arranged by the St Marylebone Public Library as a contribution to the Festival of Britain. This included a reconstruction of the sitting-room, part of which may still be seen in the Sherlock Holmes Public House.

Letters still arrive in large numbers and during my time in office Holmes has received post from ever quarter of the globe. There are fan letters, birthday wishes, Christmas cards (one each year is from Dr Watson), invitations to give lectures or attend weddings, and many other strange requests. Sometimes he learns that he is the potential winner of a fortune or that he has been specially selected to receive a trial subscription to a periodical, but by far the largest number contain details of intriguing mysteries. He is asked to trace, as it may be, a Peanut Thief in Kansas or to bring to justice the chopstick murderer of Nagasaki or to solve the arms race. Some bring news of Professor Moriarty, claiming that he has been seen boarding a train in Neasden or that he is responsible for the theft of a painting from the Dulwich Art Gallery. Others again

To cope with the hundreds of letters still addressed every year to Sherlock Holmes, the Abbey National Building Society now use a standard form of letter like this to make it easier to reply to every one.

wish to know intimate details of the detective's private life. Was he left or right-handed? Did he dislike gooseberry jam? Did he once wound Mrs Hudson in the foot while cleaing a revolver? And did Mycroft Holmes wear glasses?

These and other questions are hard to answer and I have to remind his correspondents that Holmes is now spending much of his time in Sussex and is rarely, if ever, on hand to deal with the queries himself. But I know that he appreciates all the kind comments made about him and is touched by the evidence of the high regard in which he is held.

He will always reside at 221B Baker Street, but if the Abbey National Building Society has been able to play its part in sustaining his tenancy then that is a cause for satisfaction. I certainly enjoy the work and could not wish for a better or more distinguished employer.

Best wishes.

Yours faithfully,

Sue Brown
Secretary to Sherlock Holmes

SB:VC

Who can blame Abbey National for profiting from the ceaseless interest in Sherlock Holmes? When re-building work took place, they sold old bricks from the building as souvenirs.

INDEX

Acknowledgments
The author and publisher would like
to thank the following for their help
in compiling this book: Alan Gooch
the designer, Helen Dawson for the
index, Nicki Giles for production,
and Judith Millidge for editing it.
They are also grateful to these
individuals and agencies for the use
of the illustrations on the pages
noted below:

BFI: Pages: 44; 75; 51 (both); 53
(top); 54 (top); 55 (both); 56 (both);
58; 59 (both); 62; 65; 66 (both); 67
(both); 68 (both); 71 (top); 74
(bottom right); 77; 78 (bottom two);
79 (both); 80; 81 (both); 83; 84 (top);
85 (both); 101 (top, & bottom left);
103 (both); 104 (top); 105; 106; 107
(top); 114 (top); 115; 119 (top); 120
(top); 122; 123 (both).

Bison: Pages: 98; 99; 119 (bottom).

Richard Lancelyn Green
Collection: Pages 2-3; 4-5; 7; 8; 12
(top right); 15 (right pair); 17
(bottom); 19; 20; 21 (both); 24; 26;
27; 36 (bottom); 54 (bottom); 60
(top); 82; 96 (top); 101 (bottom left);
102 (both); 104 (bottom); 107
(bottom); 109; 124; 125 (bottom); 131;
133; 134 (top); 138; 139 (top right);
148 (top & right); 150 (bottom); 152
(top); 153; 154; 155; 157.

London Transport Museum: Page
151 (both).

Stanley MacKenzie Collection:
Pages 1; 6; 9 (all three); 10; 11 (both);
12 (top left & bottom); 13 both; 14;
15; 16 (all three); 17 (top); 18 (all
three); 22 (all three); 23 (all three);
25 (both); 28 (bottom); 29 (bottom);
30; 31; 32 (top); 33; 37 (top &
bottom right); 38; 39 (both); 42; 43
(both); 46 (both); 47 (both); 73
(bottom); 100 (top); 110 (top); 112
(top); 126; 127 (all three); 128 (both);
129 (top left & bottom two); 130
(bottom); 132; 139 (top, left &
bottom two); 140 (bottom); 143; 148
(bottom); 152 (bottom); 158.

Michael Pointer Collection: 28
(top); 29 (top); 32 (bottom); 34 (all
three); 35; 36 (top); 37 (both); 40
(both); 41 (both); 47 (top); 49; 50; 52
(both); 53 (bottom); 57; 60 (bottom);
61; 63; 64 (both); 67 (top); 69; 70; 71
(bottom); 72; 73 (top); 74 (top &
bottom left); 75; 76; 78 (top); 84; 87
(both); 88; 89 (both); 90 (both); 91
(all three); 92 (both); 93; 95 (both);
96 (bottom); 97 (both); 100 (bottom);
108; 110 (bottom); 111; 112; 114
(bottom); 116 (both); 117; 118; 120
(both); 121 (bottom); 125 (top two);
129 (top right); 130 (top two); 134
(bottom); 135 (both); 138; 139 (both);
140 (top); 141; 142; 144; 145; 146; 147;
149; 150 (top).

Billy Rose Theater Collection:
Page 86.

United Features Syndicate: Page
158.